THE WAY OF CAIN

THE CREATION OF MAN'S RELIGION

By: GARY PAUL MILLER

ISBN: 978-1-60208-222-9

Published by: Grace Harbor Church
www.grace-harbor-church.org

PRINT EXECUTORS

Print Printers Inc
CITICAP CHANNELS LTD
www.printprinters.com
connect@printprinters.com

You THINK...
We PRINT !

PRINTED IN INDIA

To those who brought the story of Cain and Abel to life for me... I pray that they will obey from the heart the doctrines contained in this book and recover themselves from the error of their "way".

Author's Comments

This book came about because I always had the question as to why Cain bothered to go to the altar. I viewed him as being a rough, mean, and unbelieving man who wanted to do things his own way. So the question arose: why did he go to the altar?

This puzzling question sent me on a journey into the scriptures to find the answer. Little did I realize the impact that this one question would have on my understanding of what happened at the altar with Cain and Abel. When I learned the answer to this question, I knew I had to write a book and expose Cain for who he truly was and why he would not miss the opportunity to show up and to show off at the altar. These are important truths for all men to know and understand.

A very special thank you to my wife without whose love and support I may never have written this book. She knows the importance it will have to the Body of Christ, and her encouragement was crucial to its completion. To my father, who put in many hours examining the scriptures and was a great help in editing the book. And lastly to the saints who helped bring this book into existence.

Table of Contents

Chapter 1 – Cain Not Forgotten

Chapter 2 – In the Beginning

Chapter 3 – The Knowledge of Good and Evil

Chapter 4 – The Promise

Chapter 5 – A Man from the Lord

Chapter 6 – Into the Family Beginning

Chapter 7 – Brought Up in the Word of the Lord

Chapter 8 – Cain Prepares to Meet God

Chapter 9 – Who does Jesus Christ say Killed Abel?

Chapter 10 – The Generation of Cain

Chapter 11 – Cain's True Father: Satan

Chapter 12 – Cain: Yesterday, Today, and Tomorrow

Chapter 13 – The Two Ways

Chapter 14 – The Way of Cain

Chapter 15 – God Condemns the "Way of Cain"

Chapter 16 – Righteousness by Faith

Chapter 17 – Abel: A Prophet's offering and the fat thereof

Chapter 18 – A Witness for Abel

Chapter 19 – Cain's Sacrifice of "Good"

Chapter 20 – The Judgment of God

8

Chapter 21 – The Wrath of Cain

Chapter 22 – God's Response to Cain's Wrath

Chapter 23 – Sin Lieth at the Door

Chapter 24 – The Door

Chapter 25 – Cain the First Thief

Chapter 26 – The Killing of Abel

Chapter 27 – War with God

Chapter 28 – Cain's Deed Revealed

Chapter 29 – Blood that Speaketh

Chapter 30 – Cain's Punishment

Chapter 31 – Cain's City

Chapter 32 – Enoch: The World Religion

Chapter 33 – The End of Cain's Civilization

Chapter 34 – Conclusion

Appendix A – The Mark of Cain

Appendix B – A Defense for Adam?

Appendix C – Believers who go back to "the way of Cain"

Prov. 14:12 There is a way which seemeth right unto a man, but the end thereof are the ways of death.

Since the fall of Adam, men have sought a "way" to regain the paradise that was lost. Attaining eternal life and victory over death has been man's chief aim and goal throughout history. In man's quest for eternal bliss, a "way" has been established by which men seek to accomplish this monumental task. This "way" has been followed and traversed by countless billions, all with the hopes of grasping the prize of eternal life.

The Bible speaks of this "way", a "way" that man has devised, a "way" brought about by his own reasoning and desires. God has given a name to this "way", a name that testifies to the first man to walk in this "way". This name points to the originator and founder of this "way", a man who initially set the markers for others to follow. Thus God calls it "the way of Cain".

Jude 11a Woe unto them! for they have gone in the way of Cain

The purpose of this book is to study and expose the true person of Cain and his "way" as revealed in the scriptures. To this author's knowledge, a thorough biblical study of Cain and his "way" has never been fully undertaken. It will be my humble attempt to accomplish this because of the impact that his "way" has on mankind. Most of what has been said about Cain leaves the student without really knowing who he was. This is perilous because of God's "Woe" to those that follow Cain's "way". The pages that follow are intended to inform the reader of "the way of Cain".

CHAPTER 1

CAIN NOT FORGOTTEN

The "way of Cain" gets its name from Cain. This man is found in the book of Genesis. It is here that we find the narrative of Adam and Eve and their children, Cain and Abel.

The brothers, Cain and Abel, are two of the most recognizable brothers in history. Their lives form the basis of one of the most well known stories known to mankind. The short, yet emotional story has captured the imagination and interest of every generation. The epic battle between these brothers has permeated all cultures, races, and religions.[1] Their tale of rivalry stretches around the world. Cain's remark back to God is one of the most familiar statements in history, and most people can quote it word for word, **"Am I my brother's keeper?"**

Though the story is thousands of years old, it is still relevant today. Literature abounds with references and analogies to the struggle between Cain and Abel. From playwrights to social engineers, the story of Cain and Abel has had a lasting impact.

---

[1] Most religious writings and ancient traditions have similar stories of struggles between two brothers. Ancient Sumerian literature has the battle between Dumuzi and Enkimdu. Egyptian hieroglyphs relate a similar tale between Seth who kills his brother-in-law Osiris. The Muslim Quran has the story. It is found in Roman history through Romulus and Remus. In India there is Pandavas and Kauravas and in Persia there is the story of Ahura Mazdah and Azhi Dahaka. Even in Hawaii there is the myth of two sons who fought each other until one of them died. Each of these variations has at its source the biblical account of Cain and Abel. Every culture has been touched by the conflict of Cain and Abel.

Worldwide, Cain is known for killing his brother in a fit of rage. His actions have not been forgotten with the passage of time. Cain's rage stemmed from being rejected by God while Abel was accepted.

1 John 3:12 Not as Cain, who was of that wicked one, and slew his brother. And wherefore slew he him? Because his own works were evil, and his brother's righteous.

Men are often confused as to why God rejected Cain and accepted Abel. Was God unjust? The verse tells us that Cain slew his brother because of his own works. How did these works lead Cain to murder his brother? Was it really a battle between good and evil?

Even though Cain was a murderer, he established a "way" others have followed. A "way" that still exists. But what exactly is this "way", and why does it continue to influence society even after thousands of years?

The search for the answers must start at the beginning. We must go back to the time when God created man.

CHAPTER 2

IN THE BEGINNING

Gen. 2:7 And the LORD God formed man of the dust of the ground, and breathed into his nostrils the breath of life; and man became a living soul.

In the beginning God created man. And God put the man into the garden.

Gen. 2:8 And the LORD God planted a garden eastward in Eden; and there he put the man whom he had formed.

It was here, in the Garden of Eden, that Adam and Eve were to live, to experience the wonders of God's new world. Their life was to be filled with joy and bliss in serving the Lord their Creator. Everything around them was beautiful and picturesque. The earth bore fruit and yielded its strength as Adam and Eve lived in this paradise. The animal kingdom lived peacefully and was under the dominion of Adam. The sun provided warmth for the day while the moon lit the night sky. The Lord had set the earth in order for the benefit of mankind.

Gen. 2:16-17 And the LORD God commanded the man, saying, Of every tree of the garden thou mayest freely eat: But of the tree of the knowledge of good and evil, thou shalt not eat of it: for in the day that thou eatest thereof thou shalt surely die.

In this marvelous garden, God gave Adam a commandment. Amongst all the trees that God planted, there was one to test Adam's faithfulness. God's commandment was for Adam and Eve to not eat the fruit of one tree, the tree of the knowledge of good and evil. The Lord instructed Adam as to the consequences of breaking this commandment, **"for in the day that thou eatest therefore thou shall surely die"**. Adam knew full well to not eat of this tree, he knew the consequences, he knew to obey God.

Lurking in the shadows of the garden was another creature, a creature that had rebelled against God. A creature that was corrupt and now sought to corrupt mankind. It was this creature which first approached Eve. As the serpent revealed himself to Eve, she did not run in fear but was entranced by his beautiful words. Words which spoke of grander things, words that lifted her to new heights, words that caused her to want to be a god.

Gen. 3:4-6 And the serpent said unto the woman, Ye shall not surely die:
For God doth know that in the day ye eat thereof, then your eyes shall be opened, and ye shall be as gods, knowing good and evil. And when the woman saw that the tree was good for food, and that it was pleasant to the eyes, and a tree to be desired to make one wise, she took of the fruit thereof, and did eat, and gave also unto her husband with her; and he did eat.

Satan planted the seeds of discontent within Eve and she gave them fertile ground in her heart. Satan said that she would **"not surely die"** if she ate of the forbidden tree, but instead, she would become immortal, she would become as a god. This was the lie that Satan boasted, **"ye shalt not surely die"**. It was this lie that Eve believed. Eve's desires turned to the fruit of that tree, a tree she knew God commanded to not eat of. Seeking to be a god, she took the fruit and ate of it, and then passed it to Adam who also ate of it.

The dream of deification turned into a nightmare as they realized their shame in their nakedness. The hope that they had placed in that tree was false. It had not allowed them to reach into the heavens, to place a throne over and above God's. In their shame, they ran from the presence of the Lord, sewing fig leaves together to cover their now bare bodies.

Gen. 3:7 And the eyes of them both were opened, and they knew that they were naked; and they sewed fig leaves together, and made themselves aprons.

The Lord seeks out Adam and questions him regarding his actions. Adam, in response, blames his wife. He looks at Eve and claims it was her fault, that she made him do it. Eve in turn, blames the serpent for deceiving her.

Gen. 3:11-13 And he said, Who told thee that thou wast naked? Hast thou eaten of the tree, whereof I commanded thee that thou shouldest not eat? And the man said, The woman whom thou gavest to be with me, she gave me of the tree, and I did eat.
And the LORD God said unto the woman, What is this that thou hast done? And the woman said, The serpent beguiled me, and I did eat.

Because of their sin, the Lord pronounced judgment upon them.

Gen. 3:17-19 And unto Adam he said, Because thou hast hearkened unto the voice of thy wife, and hast eaten of the tree, of which I commanded thee, saying, Thou shalt not eat of it: cursed is the ground for thy sake; in sorrow shalt thou eat of it all the days of thy life; Thorns also and thistles shall it bring forth to thee; and thou shalt eat the herb of the field; In the sweat of thy face shalt thou eat

bread, till thou return unto the ground; for out of it wast thou taken: for dust thou art, and unto dust shalt thou return.

The Lord cursed the ground and drove Adam and Eve out from the garden. They were not to return. Now they must live outside of paradise, they must live with the consequences of their disobedience. God did not lie; death did enter the world just as He said it would.

The world around Adam and Eve was forever changed. No longer would the ground yield its strength and vitality. No longer would they be free of sickness and disease, but pain and suffering would be their companions. Death was awakened in the earth, and it spread into every area of creation. Death found a home in the weather, the oceans, and in all the animals that God had made. The tentacles of death reached everywhere, even unto the souls of men. Death now became an enemy as it slowly took life from the living, ever moving forward, growing ever stronger with the passing of time. The wondrous earth that God had created was now a prison of death from which none could escape.

It was in this world of death that Adam now had to sweat and toil for his food. The gentle earth was now hard and indifferent. Where once fruit was in abundance and easily gathered; Adam now finds decay and rot. In the midst of his crops, weeds and thistles reign. His own body begins to feel the effects of sin; aches and pains arise as his muscles toil in the ground. Sickness, rashes, and other maladies plague his once perfectly healthy body. The world did change for Adam and Eve; it was no longer the paradise that God made. There was a new taskmaster; death, and it slowly robbed them of their joyous habitation.

The curse of sin was not limited to the physical realm; it also touched their relationship with one another. The once perfect union between Adam and Eve was now corrupted by sin. The marital problems that arise in all couples began to surface. The evil heads of anger, bitterness, and deceit arose from their once innocent hearts. Instead of peace and tranquility, Adam and Eve found themselves fighting with each other in a world that was unraveling around them.

CHAPTER 3

THE KNOWLEDGE OF GOOD AND EVIL

What exactly is this knowledge that Satan sought to corrupt man with? What was the meaning and importance of the tree from which Adam and Eve ate?

When Adam was created, the Lord gave him instructions. Adam was to keep the garden. His job was to manage and handle the maintenance of the garden that God had planted. Adam knew it would be pleasing unto the Lord to obey this commandment. He knew this was good.

Gen. 2:15   And the LORD God took the man, and put him into the garden of Eden to dress it and to keep it.

The Lord also gave Adam another commandment. This commandment dealt with the tree of the knowledge of good and evil.

Gen. 2:17   But of the tree of the knowledge of good and evil, thou shalt not eat of it: for in the day that thou eatest thereof thou shalt surely die.

The Lord was very clear in His command not to eat the fruit of this tree. The Lord left no room for misunderstanding. This was a very simple rule, a rule that even a child could understand and follow. Adam knew exactly what the Lord commanded; he would have no excuse for breaking this commandment.

Adam had a clear understanding of what was good and what was evil before he ate of the tree of knowledge of good and evil. Adam knew that it was good to keep the garden. He also knew that it would be evil to eat of the tree that the Lord said not to eat of. Adam knew it would be good to obey God and evil to disobey God. Adam knew the difference between good and evil.

It is clear that this tree was not going to impart knowledge that he already had. Adam had the knowledge of what was good and what was evil before he ate of the tree. The knowledge that this tree offered must mean something different than knowing what is good and what is evil.

Declaring something good or evil was the knowledge that this tree offered. This is far different than understanding the meaning of good and evil.

Jdg: 17:6b but every man did that which was right in his own eyes.

Men can do what is right in their own eyes because they have the knowledge of this tree.

Satan said this fruit would bring man into equality with God. One attribute that belongs to God alone is that of determining what is good and evil. This tree represented who will be that authority; will it be God or man?

This tree represented who had the authority to decide what is good and what is evil. This knowledge dealt with an area that Adam was not to approach. This authority belonged only to God and was not for man to usurp.

Adam already knew from God that it was evil to eat of the tree, but that was because God had determined that it was evil. It was God who had made the judgment that eating of the tree was evil, not Adam. Adam was to obey God's judgment. But Adam wanted to be like God, he wanted to exercise his own judgments as to what is good and evil, therefore he ate of the tree.[1]

When Adam took the fruit and ate of it, he was rebelling not only against God's command not to eat of it, but also God's authority to rule. Adam was saying that God's judgments were not right or fair. "Who is God that He should make all the rules, who does He think he is! Why should I be subject to God, why should I listen to Him and obey? I can decide for myself, I don't need to be told what to do, I am a man, I can think for myself. Who is God to say this is good and that is evil, I will decide for myself what is good and what is evil." It was with this attitude that Adam took the fruit and ate of it, for God was not going to tell him what to do.

Adam wanted to make the commandments himself; he wanted to be the one to decide if something was evil or good. He wanted to be judge, ruler, and king over creation. Consequently, Adam replaced God's authority with that of his own. He removed the knowledge of God from his thinking and substituted it with this new knowledge; a knowledge where Adam will make the judgments, where man will sit on the throne, where man can reign as a god.

All men now possess this knowledge. Men are born after the image of Adam, with the knowledge that he chose. All of mankind is now corrupted by this knowledge. We are all our own gods, each deciding what is good and evil, each trying to rule over one another, each determining that our will is the one to follow. Each standing opposed to the authority of God as the true Ruler and Judge of creation. Each man saying "I will". The knowledge that this tree offered brought about a world filled with men who think they are gods, a world of violence, crime, and wars as each man seeks to thrust his

---

[1] See Appendix B

knowledge onto others. This is the fruit of that tree, the tree of the knowledge of good and evil.

Adam and Eve's sin was not a simple misunderstanding or an innocent act. It went to the heart of who is in authority, who is judge, who is ruler, and king, who will be God. Man now declares that God is no longer in charge or needed. There is a new god, and that is man himself.

CHAPTER 4

THE PROMISE

The world that Adam and Eve were created into was now ruined by their sin. With the entrance of this corrupt knowledge the earth was cursed, and the union between God and man was broken. Man was now separated from God and sentenced to death. When man rejected God, he rejected His life and without life there is nothing but death. Man's future was one of utter despair, set on a path to eternal damnation. But God did not leave man without hope, for God is a God of hope.

Rom. 15:13 Now the God of hope fill you with all joy and peace in believing, that ye may abound in hope, through the power of the Holy Ghost.

God is a God of mercies and kindness. He looks on the plight of man and is moved by His compassion and grace.

Ps. 86:15 But thou, O Lord, art a God full of compassion, and gracious, longsuffering, and plenteous in mercy and truth.

God gave Adam hope through a promise. A promise that Eve would bring forth a seed that would destroy the serpent and bring about restoration. The Lord gave a promise of a seed that would undo the curse that Adam and Eve had brought into the world. It would be through this seed that all things would be restored and made good again.

Gen. 3:15 And I will put enmity between thee and the woman, and between thy seed and her seed; it shall bruise thy head, and thou shalt bruise his heel.

God gives hope; he is a most gracious and merciful God. He removes the darkness and despair of the future and gives light and hope. He continued to love His creation, even in the face of open rebellion. He provided a wonderful promise, a promise that would result in the restitution of all things. This promise was given purely by the grace of God, for Adam did not deserve it, neither did he do anything to warrant it. Adam did not have any inherent qualities of good that caused God to make such a wonderful promise. Adam had no ground on which to stand and demand such a promise from God. It was God alone, in His infinite love that gave this promise, a promise derived from His graciousness.

This promise was a gift from God, a gift to still the consciences of Adam and Eve, a gift to ease the burden of sin and death. This gift was to provide comfort and strength in the cursed world they now found themselves. This was a most wonderful and gracious gift from God. Praise God for this gift!

Ps. 146:1 Praise ye the LORD. Praise the LORD, O my soul.

God in His mercy comforted Adam and Eve with this promise. It is to this promise that Adam and Eve must now cling, a hope that would lessen the toils of life and the pains it now brings. All was not lost, for there was hope. This hope was to enable Eve to face the future, a hope that included the destruction of the wicked serpent that had deceived her. Because of this promise, Eve knew it would be through her that the seed would come; she would bring about the promised seed.

God spoke this promise. God gives hope through His word, God's word gives power and strength to the weary, it gives hope to the hopeless, it brings comfort to the comfortless.

God's words are very important to Him and He watches over them, for it is in the words of God that we, too, find hope and salvation. The words of God are what we must trust in, to take hope, as Adam and Eve did.

Ps. 119:81 My soul fainteth for thy salvation: but I hope in thy word.

CHAPTER 5

A MAN FROM THE LORD

Adam's sin had corrupted the world bringing upon it the sentence of death. The only light in this desperate scene was the promise that God had given. This was the state of the world when Adam knew his wife, and she bare Cain.

Gen. 4:1   And Adam knew Eve his wife; and she conceived, and bare Cain, and said, I have gotten a man from the LORD.

One can learn much about Eve's expectations from her sons by the names she gave them. Cain means, "to get" versus Abel which means "vanity". And much can be learned from their occupations, Cain the farmer and Abel the shepherd.

The birth of Cain was a joyous occasion for Eve. Adam called his wife's name Eve, meaning the mother of all living, and now she did bring forth life. Through her womb she bore a son. A new life was born into this world of death. She takes her son and looks to the Lord; here in her arms is a man from the Lord, a man who is of her seed. Her mind goes back to the promise of God, that of her seed, one would come who would bring the restitution of all things.[1] Eve was trusting in

---

[1] When Eve has her third child, Seth, she again remembers God's promise.

Gen. 4:25 And Adam knew his wife again; and she bare a son, and called his name Seth: For God, said she, hath appointed me another seed instead of Abel, whom Cain slew.

This verse gives insight into the mind of Eve as to what she was thinking at the birth of her children. She was recalling the promise of the seed at the birth of her children. She was looking for the fulfillment of the promise. Eve was a faithful woman, trusting in the word of God. But by

the promise of God and readily looked for its fulfillment. She believed the promise; she had faith in God to keep His word. Without knowing the Lord's timing, she rushed ahead; believing that the promise would now be fulfilled in this first child. She looked at the child and called his name Cain.

Cain means one who will "possess", "acquire", "to get". She saw all that she lost through their sin and believed that Cain would be the one "to get" it all back. Her life would now be devoted to her son, for her son could now fulfill the promise. Cain would be the one to restore all that Adam lost. The one who would acquire the paradise that they ruined. They could not restore the world, but her seed would be able to. This is why she named him Cain; she was expecting the immediate fulfillment of God's promise.

She beamed with joy at the thought that this baby would one day crush that old serpent that had beguiled her. This would be her revenge, she had given birth to the man that would destroy the creature that brought all this pain into her life. She detested the serpent, she blamed him for the difficulties they found themselves in, and now she comforted herself in thinking that the serpent's days are numbered, for she had the seed.

This child will relieve the burden on Adam. No longer would he toil and sweat alone, Adam would have someone to help him, someone who will ease the load and weight of the cursed creation. Eve joyously looks to the Lord and thanks Him for the gift of her son. Cain would be the one to acquire

---

the time Seth was born she was aware of the fact that Cain was not the promised seed. Through the fall of Cain and the faith displayed by Abel, Eve realized that she had been greatly mistaken in her attempt to identify Cain with the promised seed. She now understood that the seed should have gone through Abel, so she calls this third child Seth, meaning " a substitute".

the paradise that they were forced to leave. It is with special promise and hope that Cain enters the world.

And she bare again.

Gen. 4:2a And she again bare his brother Abel

In addition to the glorious event of the birth of Cain, Eve had a second child. Eve's thoughts have all been about Cain and the fulfillment of the promise. When she looked upon her second son, she called his name Abel. Abel means "vanity", "useless" or "futile". As Eve compares her children, she put all of her hopes and desires into the first child, thus the name Cain. The second child is named Abel, "useless". Abel could do nothing to ease the life that Adam and Eve now live; he is useless as far as the promise is concerned. It would be through Cain, the first born, the first seed in which all hope will be placed, and therefore Abel has no hope attached to his name.

Upon the birth of Cain, Eve said she had a **"man from the Lord"**. She did not say this of Abel. In Eve's mind Cain was special, for he was from God, the promised seed. It is clearly evident that Eve's thoughts were on the promise; for this is reflected by her statement **"a man from the Lord"** and in the names she gave to her children.[2]

---

[2] After the birth of Cain, Eve has a second child named Abel. In all probability they were twins. The scriptures do not say that Adam knew Eve a second time (as it does with Seth) but it does say that she bare again, as if right after baring Cain. Also, when the time came for them to bring a sacrifice both Cain and Abel came on the same day. This would indicate that the time appointed for both boys was the same and based on the fact that they were of the same age, being twins.

CHAPTER 6

INTO THE FAMILY BUSINESS

Gen. 4:2b And Abel was a keeper of sheep, but Cain was a tiller of the ground.

There is more that can be
learned about these two
brothers from their
occupations. Adam took
Cain with him into the field
and taught Cain to till the
ground. This was Adam's
occupation, and he now
takes his son into it with
him. It brings great pride to

a father when his son joins him in the same field of work.
Cain is the one Adam will spend time with in the field,
laboring together. Cain is the one who will start the process
of relieving the burden on Adam. Cain is the one who is to
bring hope.

Abel was a keeper of sheep. He was not needed in producing
the fruit that would feed the family, for that was Cain's job.
Instead, Abel had the lowly job of a shepherd. Abel's
occupation was to wander alone with the sheep. Shepherds
spend their time away from home, in the wilderness, apart
from the family. Since Adam and Eve believed that Abel was
not the seed spoken of in the promise, they place less
importance upon him and his occupation.

We find shepherds in scripture as being overlooked and
unimportant.

David was a shepherd. The prophet Samuel is called by the Lord to go and anoint a new king over Israel. Samuel is instructed to go to the house of Jesse to find the new king.

1 Sam. 16:1 And the LORD said unto Samuel, How long wilt thou mourn for Saul, seeing I have rejected him from reigning over Israel? fill thine horn with oil, and go, I will send thee to Jesse the Bethlehemite: for I have provided me a king among his sons.

When Samuel reaches the household of Jesse, he asks that all of his sons come to the sacrifice, so he may anoint one with oil.

1 Sam. 16:5 And he said, Peaceably: I am come to sacrifice unto the LORD: sanctify yourselves, and come with me to the sacrifice. And he sanctified Jesse and his sons, and called them to the sacrifice.

Jesse makes each one of his sons to pass before Samuel. As they passed in front of Samuel the Lord rejected all of them. When none are accepted, Samuel turns to Jesse and asks if all of his sons are here. Jesse states that there is another, his youngest that is keeping the sheep.

1 Sam. 16:10-11 Again, Jesse made seven of his sons to pass before Samuel. And Samuel said unto Jesse, The LORD hath not chosen these.
And Samuel said unto Jesse, Are here all thy children? And he said, There remaineth yet the youngest, and, behold, he keepeth the sheep. And Samuel said unto Jesse, Send and fetch him: for we will not sit down till he come hither.

When Jesse was asked to gather his sons, he neglected to bring David. David was not included. He was overlooked, he was considered unimportant and without promise. David was a shepherd, an occupation for those of whom no great accomplishment was expected.

David's eldest brother ridiculed and mocked David because he was a shepherd.

1 Sam. 17:28a And Eliab his eldest brother heard when he spake unto the men; and Eliab's anger was kindled against David, and he said, Why camest thou down hither? and with whom hast thou left those few sheep in the wilderness?

The world shares this disdain for shepherds. When Joseph was going to bring his brethren unto Egypt (a type of the world) he told them to tell the Egyptians that they were not shepherds. The occupation of a shepherd was viewed as a most unworthy task and reserved for the lowest sorts of people.

Gen. 46:34 That ye shall say, Thy servants' trade hath been about cattle from our youth even until now, both we, and also our fathers: that ye may dwell in the land of Goshen; for every shepherd is an abomination unto the Egyptians.

Shepherds are soon forgotten and considered useless, they don't get respect. Abel's occupation tells us much about his parents' attitudes towards him. Abel's occupation fits perfectly with the meaning of his name, "vanity".

CHAPTER 7

BROUGHT UP IN THE WORD OF THE LORD

It was by faith that Abel brought the proper sacrifice.

Heb. 11:4a   By faith Abel offered unto God a more excellent sacrifice than Cain,

And faith can only come by hearing the word of God.

Rom. 10:17   So then faith cometh by hearing, and hearing by the word of God.

In order for Abel to have faith, God's word must have been available for him to hear. Faith can only occur by trusting in the word of God. Abel heard God's word and believed it.

God's word was accessible, to teach the "way" of God. God cared for his creation and spoke words about the need for a sacrifice. Abel did not need to guess how to please God, he knew directly from God.[1] The word of God was spoken to the first family to bring life to those who believed it.

As Adam and Eve raised their children, there would be times of discussion about the things of God. Cain and Abel were instructed in many lessons about God. They knew God existed and that He created everything. Adam could talk of the day he opened his eyes for the first time and saw his Maker, the Lord. Cain and Abel learned of the garden and how God had prepared this wonderful place for man to dwell. Adam and Eve may have taken the children on trips to visit the garden, only being allowed to come to the entrance

---

[1] More will be said on this in Chapter 17

of it. What a sight to behold, the view of the garden behind the cherubim, and the turning flaming sword.

Cain and Abel learned about the tree of the knowledge of good and evil. Conversations revolved around the serpent that beguiled their mother and deceived her into believing a lie. Much could be said of that serpent, how he proffered a knowledge that was against God, how he was an enemy of the Lord, how his goal was to be like the Most High. The serpent was a liar and to be avoided. He was not a friend of God nor should he be a friend of man. They talked of the day when the serpent would be destroyed, when that slithering snake would have its head crushed and be no more.

Cain and Abel knew of sin and the punishment it brings. The curse that God put on the earth could be seen around them. They also knew that sin had caused man's separation from God. They were taught that men are sinners and that they needed to bring a sacrifice to the Lord.

Cain and Abel could see God's mercy and graciousness in the clothing He provided for Adam and Eve after they sinned. They knew that the work of sewing fig leaves did not cover sin, but that God required blood for the remission of sins, the blood of a sacrifice.

Gen. 3:21 Unto Adam also and to his wife did the LORD God make coats of skins, and clothed them.

The Lord made the first sacrifice when He provided clothing for Adam and Eve. The Lord slew an animal and shed its blood to make the coats of skins. The Lord, in making this sacrifice, demonstrated to man the need for a sacrificial offering. Adam saw that blood was needed for the covering of sin. The Lord did not respect the aprons of fig leaves that Adam and Eve made. Cain and Able knew these truths as

Adam and Eve retold the events of that day. They could also see the coats that God had made.

The patience and longsuffering of God were apparent in that He did not immediately physically kill Adam and Eve. God could have slain them when they ate the fruit, but He did not. He gave them time, time to be saved from the terrible judgment that they brought upon themselves.[2]

Cain and Abel saw the goodness of God. The wonderful foods and sights that filled their senses spoke of a marvelous Creator. They heard the promise that God had given, how that one day all would be restored. The Lord's care and love for them could easily be understood and appreciated. Both Cain and Abel should have praised the Lord for all His blessings and love He had shown. Joyous songs should have been sung, praising God for His splendor and might. They had no excuse not to look to God for all their needs, both physically and spiritually. They knew God was worthy to be trusted and obeyed.

---

[2] God still gives man time to be saved. Death is in the physical world, but it slowly advances forward, allowing time for those caught in its grasp to find the "way" of God. God does not immediately execute final judgment on men when they sin; He withholds judgment, providing time for men to be saved. Paul is clear about how we are to use our time, to accept God's salvation.

II Cor. 6:2 (For he saith, I have heard thee in a time accepted, and in the day of salvation have I succoured thee: behold, now is the accepted time; behold, now is the day of salvation.)

CHAPTER 8

CAIN PREPARES TO MEET GOD

From the day of his birth, Cain was honored above Abel. He was honored both with his name and occupation. He was believed to be the seed that would crush the head of the serpent, the fulfiller of the promise of God. Soon the time came when he would meet God at the place of offering.

Gen. 4:3 And in process of time it came to pass, that Cain brought of the fruit of the ground an offering unto the LORD.

Much can be learned from the fact that Cain brought an offering to the Lord. Cain had the choice to appear or not to appear that day. Cain could have ignored this sacrifice, opting instead to tend to his garden or any other activity he deemed more important. But the scriptures state that Cain came on the appointed day. This demonstrated Cain's willingness and desire to appear before God. Cain wanted to meet God that day; he chose to go to the altar. He was not forced to go, but of his own free will he approached God.

Cain made great preparations well in advance for this day. **Cain decided he was going to bring God something special, something that he had done.** He brought the fruit of his hands.

Because Cain knew that he was going to bring God his fruit, he made it the best that he could. This fruit did not just spring up of its own accord. Cain put much effort into its preparation. Cain looked at all the seeds he had at his disposal and picked out the best ones. He selected the perfect location to sow his seeds and carefully prepared the soil.

After planting them he worked tirelessly, watering and watching over them. He pulled the weeds and thistles that tried to get in the way of his fruit. He pruned the plants so that they each produced the best they could grow. This was a laborious job, but one that Cain readily accepted as he was determined to bring a beautiful offering unto the Lord.[1]

Cain's attendance to and production of his fruit gives insight to his true identity. He was a man that knew about God. He desired to be praised by God and he established a "way" to accomplish that. He toiled in his works, producing the best he could. He was not distracted or negligent in his efforts. He gave his all to this fruit right up to the day that he picked and readied it. With his fruit in hand, he went to the altar before God on the appointed day. What is becoming clear is that Cain was a hard workman, a man who was laboring to be praised by the Lord.

Cain's actions demonstrate that he was a religious man. He wanted to do the best he could for God, that's what a religious man does. We know he was not an atheist who didn't believe in the existence of God. He was instead a man deeply devoted to his work, seeking to prove to God just how good he was. His tireless labor in growing this fruit clearly displays his zeal for God. Cain was driven by religious fervor in his determination to approach God with his best offering. Thus the true character of Cain is starting to be revealed, he was a passionate religious man.

We have seen significant insight into who Cain was, from his name, to his occupation, to his tireless work. However, in the next chapter, we will learn even more in looking at what the Lord Jesus Christ said to the Pharisees about the "person"

---

[1] We know this to be true based on who Cain really was, which will be covered in Chapter 9.

who killed Abel.

CHAPTER 9

WHO DOES THE LORD JESUS CHRIST
SAY KILLED ABEL?

Cain's true identity is coming to light by understanding his attempt to appease God through his own efforts of growing fruit of the ground. The activity undertaken by Cain clearly demonstrates he was a religious man, devoted to his work. But there is more to Cain's zealousness that the Lord Jesus Christ states. The account in Genesis must be left for a moment as we turn to the ministry of Jesus Christ when He was on the earth.

God wrote the Bible progressively, meaning more is revealed as one advances further into the Book. Scripture is built upon scripture, and additional truth can be learned of past events from this further revelation. Such is the case with Cain and Abel. It is not until we come to the Lord Jesus Christ that more facts are given as to the character of these men.

Jesus Christ only makes two references to Cain and Abel, once in Matthew and once in Luke. It is from these further revelations, that the Bible student can learn more about each of these men.

Jesus Christ makes reference to the murder of Abel when speaking with the Pharisees. Before we uncover the true identity of the person Jesus Christ says killed Abel, let us examine the men that Christ was speaking to, the Pharisees.

Jesus Christ describes Pharisees as religious men, seeking to gain the favor of men. Pharisees hope to gain eternal life through their own good works and self-righteousness. They live pious lives, placing their trust in themselves, seeking to trade their good deeds for a place in the kingdom of God.

Matt. 23:5-7 But all their works they do for to be seen of men: they make broad their phylacteries, and enlarge the borders of their garments,
And love the uppermost rooms at feasts, and the chief seats in the synagogues,
And greetings in the markets, and to be called of men, Rabbi, Rabbi.

Pharisees publicly display their works for others to see. They seek the adoration of men. Their works are not done in private, but are paraded for all to hear and see. These men are consumed with being praised by others, praised for their good works. They wear their good deeds on their clothing, attaching to themselves proofs of their great religious accomplishments.

Matt. 23:8 But be not ye called Rabbi: for one is your Master, even Christ; and all ye are brethren.

One of the goals of these religious men was to attain the title of Rabbi. This position was one of a Master, Teacher, one who was over others in spiritual matters. Much like men today who want the religious title of Father, Priest, Mullah, Imam, or Dali Lama. Men have dominion over others by using these titles.

Jesus Christ states that there is only one Master. The position and title of Rabbi was reserved for Christ himself. It is not a title that men could steal and label themselves with. There is one Master, one Rabbi, one Christ, all others are counterfeits and false.

Matt. 23:13 But woe unto you, scribes and Pharisees, hypocrites! for ye shut up the kingdom of heaven against

men: for ye neither go in yourselves, neither suffer ye them that are entering to go in.

Through their efforts to elevate themselves, they remove Christ as the true Rabbi and insert themselves. These men are seeking their own glory, their own place on a pedestal, one without God. They stand in the "way", taking the place of Jesus Christ. Pharisees stand against Christ, barring the "way" of entering into the kingdom. They have shut the "way" of entrance by offering another "way", a "way" that will not lead to the kingdom but to hell itself. They may speak of the kingdom and say they know the "way" but they do not.

Pharisees deceive men into following them and not the Lord Jesus Christ. They try and entrap those wanting to enter into the kingdom; they set snares and traps to prevent the true "way". They are hypocrites, professing to show the open gates of the kingdom, but in reality they hold open the doors leading to torment and fire.

Matt. 23:14   Woe unto you, scribes and Pharisees, hypocrites! for ye devour widows' houses, and for a pretence make long prayer: therefore ye shall receive the greater damnation.

Pharisees are known for making long prayers. They appear devout and godly by their prayers. These prayers are not said in a corner but in public for all to witness. Men would ask Pharisees to pray for them, to appeal to God for them. These priests would pray for hours, or many times a day, appearing to be making intercession for those they prayed for. They would receive large sums of money from widows in exchange for their prayers. The Lord knew it was all done as a pretense, as a way of taking money from the masses, a way of holding their position of power over people. "Pay to Pray" is the Pharisee mantra, but the Lord would have none of it. Thus the Lord pronounces **"Woe"** unto these men.

Matt. 23:15   Woe unto you, scribes and Pharisees, hypocrites! for ye compass sea and land to make one proselyte, and when he is made, ye make him twofold more the child of hell than yourselves.

Hypocrites are what Christ calls them, devilish men, traitors to the true "way" of God. The men who had the religious titles and training, the men who prayed long public prayers, the men who said they know the "way" to the kingdom, it was these men that Christ called hypocrites. They seemed like holy men of God but they were only actors, putting on a show, feigning righteousness. Their appearance as highly devout men was false, they were not who they claimed to be. Jesus Christ calls them what they truly were, hypocrites.

Pharisees seek men to follow them, men who place their trust in what they have to say. They would diligently search the whole world, looking for proselytes, recruits. Pharisees are not bashful about their religion or works, they are not afraid to speak boldly, hoping to convert those around them.

Hell is their destination, and not the kingdom of God. They say they lead the way to paradise, but they are lost. Their end shall be the same as that of the Devil and his demons. No green pastures or honey to taste, instead they shall have fire and brimstone fed to them as they waste together in hell.

Matt. 23:16   Woe unto you, ye blind guides, which say, Whosoever shall swear by the temple, it is nothing; but whosoever shall swear by the gold of the temple, he is a debtor!

Pharisees are blind. Who would follow a blind man down a

trail? Who would commit their safety, their lives to one who cannot see? They offer themselves as guides to eternal life and bliss; but they cannot even see their own nose, much less the kingdom. Instead of groping alone in the dark, Pharisees have many followers who line up behind and go where they are led. As sheep to the slaughter, so men's souls are being lead to Hell.

Matt. 23:25-28   Woe unto you, scribes and Pharisees, hypocrites! for ye make clean the outside of the cup and of the platter, but within they are full of extortion and excess.
Thou blind Pharisee, cleanse first that which is within the cup and platter, that the outside of them may be clean also.
Woe unto you, scribes and Pharisees, hypocrites! for ye are like unto whited sepulchres, which indeed appear beautiful outward, but are within full of dead men's bones, and of all uncleanness.
Even so ye also outwardly appear righteous unto men, but within ye are full of hypocrisy and iniquity.

A Pharisee appears clean on the outside, he looks godly in appearance. He goes to great efforts to separate himself from any hint of impropriety. Some would not even eat with publicans or sinners, washing themselves clean from the filth of society. They created another class, a class that was above the common man, a class unto themselves, a class of holy men, comprised of the best and most learned. They seek to surpass others in good deeds and manner of life. They wore long religious robes and carried their holy books, abstaining from all appearance of evil.

A walk through the local morgue would reveal just what Jesus Christ expresses when talking with the Pharisees. He stated that they were dead on the inside and yet they had painted the outside to look alive, but there was truly no life within them. In spite of all their show and glitter they are still filthy and rotten. They are dead to the core, smothered with maggots of their own iniquity. They are deceivers and imitators, for their hearts are unclean, caked with the sin of pride.

Pharisees believe that through their acts of worship they will be declared righteous, they cling to their precious works. Christ knew that in their sin-blackened hearts they were full of pride, boasting of themselves against God. They had rejected the council of God that all men are sinners, that all men are spiritually dead, and that all men need a Saviour.

Some may say, "Yes, I understand what a Pharisee is. He is a hypocrite, appearing good and holy but he, in reality, is blasphemous and hates God. But what does this have to do with Cain?" The Lord Jesus Christ will now make the connection.

Matt. 23:35-36   That upon you may come all the righteous blood shed upon the earth, from the blood of righteous Abel unto the blood of Zacharias son of Barachias, whom ye slew between the temple and the altar.
Verily I say unto you, All these things shall come upon this generation.

Jesus Christ states that all Pharisees are murderers and will be found guilty of murder. Pharisees are not only evil in their heart but they are also murderers. Christ lays at the feet of the Pharisees the blood of all righteous men. Pharisees will be held responsible for all the righteous blood that has been shed on the earth. These men who have appeared saintly and godly are really murderers, they have spilt the blood of all the saints, beginning with Abel.

It is in this verse that Jesus Christ reveals who killed Abel. We learn in this verse from our Lord that a Pharisee killed Abel and committed the first murder, killing God's righteous saint. Notice in Matthew 23:35 the words **"ye slew"**. The Pharisees are the **"ye"** that Christ identifies as the murderers of His righteous. Christ goes all the way back to the slaying of Abel when He says to the Pharisees, **"ye slew"**. **Christ says a Pharisee killed Abel and Pharisees will be held accountable for Abel's blood.** The words of Christ ring out, **"ye** (Pharisees) **slew"** Abel, **"ye** (Pharisees) **slew"** Zacharias, **"ye** (Pharisees) **slew"** all the saints. Yes, Pharisees are murderers and shedders of men's blood beginning when **"ye slew"** Abel.

Jesus Christ knew full well the account in Genesis where the scriptures state that Cain killed Abel. And now in Matthew, when talking with the Pharisees, He sheds more light on Cain, revealing him to be a Pharisee. This leads to only one conclusion. **The Lord Jesus Christ is identifying Cain as a Pharisee.**

The Pharisee that killed Abel is none other than Cain himself. Christ reveals the true character of Cain, that of a Pharisee. This statement by Jesus Christ clarifies just who Cain was, a Pharisee.

This is also repeated in Luke.

**Luke 11:50-51 That the blood of all the prophets, which was shed from the foundation of the world, may be required of this generation;
From the blood of Abel unto the blood of Zacharias, which perished between the altar and the temple: verily I say unto you, It shall be required of this generation.**

More will be said about **"this generation"** referring to

Pharisees in the next chapter.

This may come as a shock to most people. Cain did not appear as an unsightly, base creature given to crude vices and filth as portrayed in the minds of many today. He instead had transformed himself into an angel of light, a minister of self-goodness and self-righteousness, a Pharisee.

Christ attributed to Cain all the characteristics of a Pharisee. The heart of Cain was no different than the hearts of the Pharisees in the Lord's day, or those in our day. Just as Pharisees seek righteousness through their own works, so did Cain. Just as Pharisees seek to reach into heaven and obtain life through their own holiness, so did Cain. Cain was a religious man who sought to please God through his own good fruit just like the Pharisees. Cain cleaned up the outside but was dead on the inside, just like all Pharisees.

Great efforts have been made by Cain's followers to keep Cain's true identity a secret. If men knew that their religious leaders are of the same mold as Cain, that the man leading the religious service in most places of worship is no different than Cain, men would hopefully flee in fear, seeking escape from these murderers. This is why Cain's identity has been masked and buried, so that he will not be recognized for who he truly is. The religious system has obscured his identity making it difficult to identify their true founder. Religion does not want the masses to know or understand that Cain was the first Pharisee, the first religious man, and that Cain's followers are ministering to them. Thus it has been that Cain the Pharisee has been hid from the public's eye. The true identity of Cain, the religious man, is not to be seen.

CHAPTER 10

THE GENERATION OF CAIN

Cain was the firstborn among men, the first to open the womb, the first to be held in his mother's arms. In addition to this, we just stated a much lesser known fact of scripture: Cain was the first Pharisee. He was the first to look for another "way", the first to seek God through his own works, the first to set up a system of worship based on his good works. Cain was the head of the Pharisees, being the first. He begins a long line of Pharisees, "this generation", that would follow after him.

Matt. 23:35-36   That upon you may come all the righteous blood shed upon the earth, from the blood of righteous Abel unto the blood of Zacharias son of Barachias, whom ye slew between the temple and the altar.
Verily I say unto you, All these things shall come upon this generation.

Luke 11:50-51 That the blood of all the prophets, which was shed from the foundation of the world, may be required of this generation;
From the blood of Abel unto the blood of Zacharias, which perished between the altar and the temple: verily I say unto you, It shall be required of this generation.

Jesus Christ lays all the righteous blood that has been shed on the earth at the feet of the Pharisees. The judgment of God against these murderous acts will come upon the "generation" of Pharisees. But what exactly does the Lord mean when He uses the word "generation" and how does this reflect on Cain?

The word generation can have many different meanings. In its most common usage it denotes those who are born to their parents, of natural lineage, or descendents. For example, the natural lineage of Jesus Christ is given in Matthew.

Matt. 1:1 The book of the generation of Jesus Christ, the son of David, the son of Abraham.

In Matthew 1:1 the word "generation" has the natural line of Jesus Christ in view. He was born from this traceable line of descendents. The natural lineage is the meaning of the word "generation" in this context.

When Jesus Christ spoke to the Pharisees in Matthew 23 and in Luke 11, He was speaking to a diverse group of Pharisees. These Pharisees were not all from the same natural lineage. Many of them were from different parents. This being the case, the most common definition of the word "generation" does not fit in this context.

The word generation sometimes refers to a group of people who live at the same time, such as the "baby boomer" generation. This meaning cannot apply because God's judgment did not fall on the Pharisees that were in His immediate presence. These Pharisees who stood in front of the Lord died without experiencing this judgment.

There is another meaning to the word "generation" which brings understanding to the word, "generation" as the Lord uses it in these passages. Here the word "generation" refers to those who belong to a certain group, who are similar in thought and belief, those who are related by way of actions or faith.

God uses the word "generation" in this way many times in scripture. For example, God has a "generation" populated by men of faith, men who have been declared righteous. All who are in this generation are related one to another because God has declared them righteous. This "generation" of the righteous is ongoing and added to daily, as men come to Jesus Christ through faith. This "generation" spans all of time and is not natural but spiritual.

Ps. 14:5 There were they in great fear: for God is in the generation of the righteous.

Ps. 112:2   His seed shall be mighty upon earth: the generation of the upright shall be blessed.

Ps. 24:6   This is the generation of them that seek him, that seek thy face, O Jacob. Selah.

Jesus Christ used this meaning of the word "generation" when He spoke with the Pharisees. During His conversation, Christ talked about all those who make up the "generation" of Pharisees beginning with Cain, and not just those in his immediate presence. Christ has the whole spiritual lineage in view, all the Pharisees, from the first to the last.

This generation of Pharisees traces its lineage all the way back to Cain, the murderer of Abel. Cain was the first Pharisee and all those who have followed are part of his generation. If one were to draw a family tree of Cain's generation of Pharisees, Cain would be at the start with all others branching off from him. Every Pharisee that has ever lived or will live is a part of this spiritual generation of which Christ spoke.

48

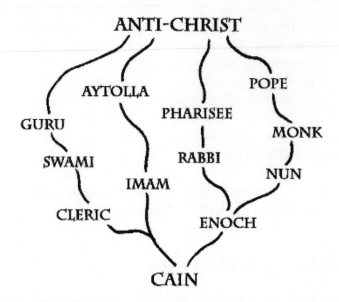

It was Cain the Pharisee that killed Abel. It was the Pharisees who killed Zacharias. It was the Pharisees who eventually killed Jesus Christ; all of these men are of the same "generation". They are all related; they are of Cain's generation. Jesus Christ attributes all the righteous blood shed upon the earth to the generation of Pharisees. He was indicting all of them, condemning all Pharisees, from the beginning to the end.

This evil generation is described in Proverbs. It is one that is rebellious and murderous. It is filled with those who are self-righteous, puffed up with their own goodness. The description of this generation matches the description of the Pharisees by the Lord Jesus Christ. This generation is spiritual and continues to grow even through our day.

Prov. 30:11-14 There is a generation that curseth their father, and doth not bless their mother.
There is a generation that are pure in their own eyes, and yet is not washed from their filthiness.

There is a generation, O how lofty are their eyes! and their eyelids are lifted up.
There is a generation, whose teeth are as swords, and their jaw teeth as knives, to devour the poor from off the earth, and the needy from among men.

The Lord Jesus Christ is waiting to judge this "generation". Each Pharisee in this "generation" will be held guilty for all the blood that has been shed against God's people. Jesus Christ holds all Pharisees accountable for their war against His saints. Every person who makes himself a member of Cain's generation will be charged with murder and fall under the judgment of God. According to Jesus Christ, every Pharisee is a murderer and guilty of shedding the blood of righteous men. This is a powerful indictment by the Lord against these men.

Pharisees exist today who are under this same judgment. They are called by different names: Your Holiness, Reverend Father, Your Piety, Your Grace, Your Eminence, Mother, Ecumenical Patriarch, Guru, Shaman, Swami, Vicar, Imam, Cardinal, etc., but they are Pharisees nonetheless. These people do testify that they are Pharisees because they seek to enter heaven by their own goodness; they preach a gospel of human effort and human good. They deny the blood of Christ as effectual, as they seek to save themselves by their own strength. They are righteous in the eyes of world. They are the same and no different than Cain the murderer, and they all will be judged guilty as murderers.

With Cain being the first in this generation, he set the standard that others follow. He was the first to approach God with his good works, the first to seek a "way", the first to become angry against God, the first to persecute the righteous, the first to kill the righteous. Yes, Cain established the "way" that all other Pharisees follow, he set the mark to which others have tried to attain, he is the forger of this wicked "way".

Cain's generation isn't the only generation spoken of in the Bible. The Bible speaks of another generation, a generation different than Cain's. There is a generation of the righteous, men whom God has declared righteous. This generation is made up of men who have sought the Lord, who have believed God, who have placed their faith in the word of God.

Ps. 112:2   His seed shall be mighty upon earth: the generation of the upright shall be blessed.

Ps. 24:6   This is the generation of them that seek him, that seek thy face, O Jacob. Selah.

Ps. 22:30   A seed shall serve him; it shall be accounted to the Lord for a generation.

Ps. 14:5   There were they in great fear: for God is in the generation of the righteous.

This righteous, spiritual generation is ongoing and continues to grow, as men trust in the Lord Jesus Christ and the work He accomplished for man on the cross.

This generation of the righteous stands opposed to the generation of Cain. It stands with God, in the light of His word, not in the darkness and corruption of Cain's generation. These two generations are contrary to one another, complete opposites. The righteous generation trusts in God while Cain's generation trusts in its own works. One is filled with the righteousness of God while the other is filled with its own righteousness. One is with Christ and his saints while the other has joined with Satan and his demons in rebellion against God. The righteous generation has the preaching of the gospel of Christ; Cain's preaches a gospel of human wisdom founded on the tree of the knowledge of good and evil. The war between these two generations started with Cain and has continued down through time. This war will persist until Christ returns in vengeance taking judgment on the evil generation of Cain.

II Thess. 1:7-9 And to you who are troubled rest with us, when the Lord Jesus shall be revealed from heaven with his mighty angels,
In flaming fire taking vengeance on them that know not God, and that obey not the gospel of our Lord Jesus Christ:
Who shall be punished with everlasting destruction from the presence of the Lord, and from the glory of his power;

Jude 11a Woe unto them! for they have gone in the way of Cain,

CHAPTER 11

CAIN'S FATHER: SATAN

Gen. 3:15 And I will put enmity between thee and the woman, and between thy seed and her seed; it shall bruise thy head, and thou shalt bruise his heel.

When God spoke this to Eve, He spoke of two seed lines. There is a seed line that God would use to bring about the bruising of the serpent's head, the ultimate destruction of Satan. There is another seed line, a seed of the serpent. God is the head of one seed line while Satan is the head of the other. Satan would have his own seed line, a seed by which he would attempt to overthrow God and usurp His throne.

Isa. 14:14 I will ascend above the heights of the clouds; I will be like the most High.

The seed line that God would work through has been declared throughout scripture. This line started with Abel, but after his death it was transferred to Seth. God continued it through Noah, Abraham, Jacob, David, and eventually to Jesus Christ. God carefully watched over this seed line.

The Devil attacked God's seed line beginning with the murder of Abel. Satan thought that if he could destroy this seed line, then God would be unable to fulfill the prophecy of Genesis 3:15. It was through this line that Jesus Christ was born. The genealogy of Jesus Christ is recorded in Matthew and Luke. He was of the seed that was promised to Eve; He would be the one to destroy the serpent and redeem man.

The serpent was to have his own seed line upon the earth,

"and between thy seed and her seed". This seed line of Satan began with Cain.

I John 3:12a Not as Cain, who was of that wicked one, and slew his brother.

Cain **"was of that wicked one"**, Satan. Cain was the other seed spoken of in Genesis 3:15. Cain believed the lie that Satan spoke to Eve, **"Ye shall not surely die"**. Cain believed the words of the Devil and not the words of God.

Gen. 3:4 And the serpent said unto the woman, Ye shall not surely die:

This is the lie that Cain believed. He could save himself; he was not going to die the second death. He was going to be his own god, giving himself life through his own works. Cain rejected the truth of God and replaced it with his own natural understanding, human wisdom. Cain declared God a liar and himself the truth. Just as Satan did not stand in the truth, so Cain does not stand in the truth. **Those that follow Cain believe the lie that they will not die, they will live forever, that they will earn eternal life. This is the lie that is at the center of all religion.** This is the lie that all Pharisees proclaim, "Be good and live! You shall not surely die!"

This is the lie that the righteous oppose, that man will not die. This lie is to be fought with the word of God. Believers battle this enemy with the sword of the Spirit, for man will die, once physically and then the second death.

Heb. 9:27 And as it is appointed unto men once to die, but after this the judgment:

Rev. 21:8 But the fearful, and unbelieving, and the

abominable, and murderers, and whoremongers, and sorcerers, and idolaters, and all liars, shall have their part in the lake which burneth with fire and brimstone: which is the second death.

Do not be like Cain and his followers; do not trust in the lie of Satan. Your eternal future is determined by who you trust. Trust in God and His word; believe that Jesus Christ shed His blood for the remission of sins. Believe that Christ rose from the grave and offers salvation as a free gift to you. Rejection of God's free gift of salvation results in you experiencing the second death, and you will burn with Cain in the Lake of Fire, for all eternity along with all the other Pharisees.

Adam was Cain's physical father but Satan became Cain's spiritual father when he believed the lie. Just as Cain emerged from the heart of Satan, so do all Pharisees. When Jesus Christ talked with the Pharisees, they proudly proclaimed that Abraham was their father.

John 8:39 They answered and said unto him, Abraham is our father. Jesus saith unto them, If ye were Abraham's children, ye would do the works of Abraham.

Yes, they were of Abraham's fleshly genealogy, but Christ knew that they had another father, a spiritual father. It was this spiritual father, Satan, which they obeyed.

John 8:44 Ye are of your father the devil, and the lusts of your father ye will do. He was a murderer from the beginning, and abode not in the truth, because there is no truth in him. When he speaketh a lie, he speaketh of his own: for he is a liar, and the father of it.

Jesus Christ spoke of Satan as the true father of the

Pharisees. The Pharisees are the children of the Devil, just as Cain was. Just as Satan was a murderer from the beginning so was Cain, and so are all Pharisees. Just as Satan hates the truth of God, so did Cain, and so do all Pharisees. Just as Satan speaks of the lie so does Cain and all Pharisees. Yes, Satan is their father; Satan has a seed that he uses to promote his lie. This seed began with Cain and continues, including all religious men who preach the lie.

In summary, Cain's religious character is exemplified by his meticulous attention to detail in bringing his fruit offering. The words of Christ testify that Cain was the first Pharisee. And Jesus Christ again links Cain and the Pharisees as all being in the same family, the family of the Devil, Satan himself. **The scriptures have shown Cain's true identity for all to see, for he was a Pharisee.**

CHAPTER 12

CAIN: YESTERDAY, TODAY, AND TOMORROW

We have learned from the scriptures that there is a rebellious generation that started with Cain. This generation continues through our day and will continue to the end times. All men who rebel against God follow the "way" set by Cain. This evil generation is alive and well, and it's all around us. In fact, we read of this generation in the book of Jude.

Jude 11a Woe unto them! for they have gone in the way of Cain,

Jude writes, warning believing Israel, that there will be those who follow after Cain. The book of Jude provides guidance to those going through the tribulation. The tribulation, being yet future, proves that Cain's "way" will still be active and flourishing up through the time of Jacob's trouble.

Jude 4 For there are certain men crept in unawares, who were before of old ordained to this condemnation, ungodly men, turning the grace of our God into lasciviousness, and denying the only Lord God, and our Lord Jesus Christ.

Jude is sounding the alarm to believing Israel that there are ungodly men amongst them. These men do not openly proclaim who they really are, but they have hidden themselves amongst the brethren, men who have crept in as wolves in sheep's clothing. These men need to be identified and removed. These are dangerous men, men who are devilish. They have come in as predators on the hunt, hoping to remain hidden until they pounce and devour. The saints had not been discerning but had permitted them to be in their midst. The followers of Cain are good at imitating godliness;

their hypocrisy makes it hard to distinguish them from godly men. Jude attempts to awaken God's saints and remove the masks of these hypocrites and show them for who they are.

These ungodly men are no different than the ungodly men of old. The men who follow Cain today are of the same generation as those in ages past. This is because Cain's "way" did not die out at the flood. The flood of Noah did not wash away the remnants of Cain's generation and Cain's "way". It survived the flood, crossing into the world today to once again bare evil fruit. Just as there were those that followed in Cain's footsteps before the flood, there are men who are following in those same footsteps now.

These men have no regard for the Lord Jesus Christ. They do not believe Him to be God; they do not look to Him for salvation. They in fact deny the Godhead, placing Christ in a position beneath God the Father. They speak of Christ with magnificent words, but they do not worship Him as God. They claim to know Christ but their faith is in their own self-righteousness. What belongs to Christ, such as forgiveness of sins, grace, peace, and eternal life; they thieve and claim for themselves. These men are wicked and repulsive. They will only destroy and corrupt the faith, leading men away from Christ. This is the venom that they seek to poison people with, the poison that denies who Jesus Christ is.

Jude points to the condemnation that awaits these men, a condemnation that has been declared against them from old. This is the same judgment that Jesus Christ warned the Pharisees about in Matthew 23 and Luke 11. God will bring His judgment, find all these wicked men guilty, and condemn them to the Lake of Fire. This is the condemnation that God has declared against those that refuse to trust His Son Jesus Christ. The "way of Cain" was condemned from the beginning, and God is still condemning it.

Jude 8-9 Likewise also these filthy dreamers defile the flesh, despise dominion, and speak evil of dignities.
Yet Michael the archangel, when contending with the devil he disputed about the body of Moses, durst not bring against him a railing accusation, but said, The Lord rebuke thee.

Jude calls them filthy dreamers, men whose imaginations are wicked. This is much like in the days of Noah where men's minds and imaginations were given over to sinful thoughts continuously.

Gen. 6:5 And GOD saw that the wickedness of man was great in the earth, and that every imagination of the thoughts of his heart was only evil continually.

In their dreams, they have elevated themselves above all forms of authority. They picture themselves sitting in high places as rulers and gods. The only authority they respect is that of their own wicked heart. They have rejected God's rule.

Jude states that even the great archangel Michael submits to God's authority. But these filthy dreamers imagine they are mightier and wiser then Michael the archangel, they do not need to submit as Michael does. Through their own imaginations they have removed God and His authority over creation and replaced the Creator with themselves.

Jude 10 But these speak evil of those things which they know not: but what they know naturally, as brute beasts, in those things they corrupt themselves.

The knowledge that these men hold is not from God, but what they know naturally. They listen to their own hearts and have shut out the knowledge of God. Proclaiming to have wisdom about life, death, sin, and salvation. They give speeches, professing their own knowledge to be wise and powerful. They talk of God, the Devil, and righteousness as if they have understanding. But here Jude exclaims they know nothing, they do not have understanding in any of these matters, and their knowledge is not from God. Jude knows that without God, one has as much understanding in these truths as an animal would have. One would be foolish to listen to a "beast" expound on love, hate, grace, or forgiveness. Cain's followers are such beasts.

Jude 11 Woe unto them! for they have gone in the way of Cain, and ran greedily after the error of Balaam for reward, and perished in the gainsaying of Core.

Jude finally exposes these ungodly men for who they really are, followers of Cain. With this verse, **Jude openly declares the real identity of the filthy dreamers; of those who are beastly in their understanding, of those who have crept in unawares, of those who have been condemned, they are all of Cain.** They walk in his "way". These evil men are filled with the spirit of Cain. This is why Jude rages the way he does. He is warning these saints that Cain is among them. Jude would not use such powerful words if he were not trying to impress them of this great danger. The men who have crept in are of the "way of Cain"!

What Cain started has lasted thousands of years. It has drawn billions of men as followers. They are walking the same path that Cain established, the same "way" of wickedness. They may secretly hide among the saints, seeking to destroy the truly righteous. They use religion as their cloak, holiness as a shroud, good works as a covering, but underneath they are dead and ungodly. Jude writes to warn the true believers of this danger.

Jude pronounces **"Woe unto them"**, **"Woe"** to these men who are ungodly, **"Woe"** unto those who follow Cain. Jesus Christ used the same word when He was speaking to the Pharisees in Matthew 23 and Luke 11. The men who are following Cain in Jude are no different than the men to whom Christ spoke. They are the same, no different than Cain.

Jude 12-13   These are spots in your feasts of charity, when they feast with you, feeding themselves without fear: clouds they are without water, carried about of winds; trees whose fruit withereth, without fruit, twice dead, plucked up by the roots;
Raging waves of the sea, foaming out their own shame; wandering stars, to whom is reserved the blackness of darkness for ever.

The followers of Cain are eating and having fellowship together with the saints. These imposters seem charitable, but beware; they are selfish, only seeking the lust of their own heart.

These ungodly men produce fruit; they think their fruit is unto everlasting life. Jude does not see their fruit this way nor is he blinded as to the real nature of their fruit. Their fruit is not what they claim it to be, for it is dead. They are as trees that have been uprooted, decaying in the noonday sun. What they offer as fruit stinks and is rotten. It is corrupted and withered. They try to make it appear good and righteous but it is only filled with maggots and wickedness.

When Cain offered his fruit to the Lord, Cain was pleased with it. But God saw something different. He didn't see goodness or holiness in the fruit of Cain. Instead, He saw in Cain a tree that had been uprooted and killed by sin. His fruit was neither holy nor righteous, there was no life giving merit in that fruit, it was dead! **This is what God saw as He looked upon the offering of Cain, He saw useless, withered, dead fruit.**

Cain's fruit does not bring life; it brings death, the second death, **"twice dead"**. Those who place their trust in this fruit will die the second death. They will be condemned to the Lake of Fire, for they have rejected the grace of God. Cain's fruit cannot bring life; it does not quicken the spirit. It does not provide salvation. **Man does not only die once physically, but he will also die a second death if he trusts in his own fruit.** Thus Cain's fruit is judged **"twice dead"**.

The judgment against these men is dreadful. They reject the light of God and abide in darkness and nothing but more darkness awaits them. It is a terrible thing to fall into the hands of the living God, One whom they have rejected and cursed.

Heb. 10:31 It is a fearful thing to fall into the hands of the living God.

This judgment is eternal damnation, and is forever. An eternity of darkness awaits these men, an eternity of suffering and separation from God. Brimstone and fire will be their end in the Lake of Fire. The severity of the judgment against the "way of Cain" should cause men to run from this evil "way". Men need to be aware of this corrupt "way of Cain" so that they do not fall under God's judgment.

Jude 16 These are murmurers, complainers, walking after their own lusts; and their mouth speaketh great swelling words, having men's persons in admiration because of advantage.

Ungodly men murmur against God and those in righteous authority, just as the Jews did against Moses in the wilderness. The Pharisees murmured against Jesus and his disciples, inciting rebellion against God and his Anointed.

Luke 5:30 But their scribes and Pharisees murmured against his disciples, saying, Why do ye eat and drink with publicans and sinners?

These murmurers follow their own lusts of the flesh. It is these lusts that they seek to fulfill.

Jude 17-19 But, beloved, remember ye the words which were spoken before of the apostles of our Lord Jesus Christ;
How that they told you there should be mockers in the last time, who should walk after their own ungodly lusts.
These be they who separate themselves, sensual, having not the Spirit.

Jude is not the only person who warns of these ungodly men. Jude states that others have warned of these wolves that have dressed themselves as sheep. Other apostles have also spoken the same; they knew there would be followers of Cain still selling Cain's fruit.

These ungodly men mock God, saying there will be no judgment. They say they will reign forever. They ask in contempt, "Where is this God? He must be away or is a liar, we have not heard from Him for many a year. The world is the same today as it was yesterday; there will be no doom for men. He speaks of judgment to scare us, but there is no power behind His words." **"Woe"** unto those that mock God, for whatsoever God speaks, that He will do.

Isa. 46:10-11 Declaring the end from the beginning, and

from ancient times the things that are not yet done, saying, My counsel shall stand, and I will do all my pleasure:
Calling a ravenous bird from the east, the man that executeth my counsel from a far country: yea, I have spoken it, I will also bring it to pass; I have purposed it, I will also do it.

One should not view God's longsuffering as reason to believe that judgment will not come.

II Pet. 3:9 The Lord is not slack concerning his promise, as some men count slackness; but is longsuffering to us-ward, not willing that any should perish, but that all should come to repentance.

The world mocked God before the flood of Noah. As Noah preached of the impending judgment, the men of that world ridiculed him. They continued to live how they always had, in the lusts of their flesh. They rejected the warnings of Noah. But God is true, and God does not lie. What He speaks that He will do, and He did flood the world with water, destroying all those that had mocked Him. The same is true of the judgment that awaits those that walk in the "way of Cain". Therefore God will fulfill His **"Woe"** unto all those who walk after Cain.

CHAPTER 13

THE TWO WAYS

The Bible speaks of only two "ways", two separate and distinct paths which mankind can follow. Both "ways" claim to lead to eternal life.

There is one "way" that God has designed. A "way" that leads to man's reconciliation and eternal life. It is through God's ordained "way" that God can declare men righteous. But there is a second "way" that men follow, the "way of Cain".

Ps. 1:6 For the LORD knoweth the way of the righteous: but the way of the ungodly shall perish.

It is only God's "way" that leads to righteousness, to eternal life. Those who choose to follow another "way" will meet with destruction. For the Lord's "way" is perfect.

Ps. 18:30 As for God, his way is perfect: the word of the LORD is tried: he is a buckler to all those that trust in him.

Thus some men have called upon God to show them the true and right path to follow.

Ex. 33:13 Now therefore, I pray thee, if I have found grace in thy sight, shew me now thy way, that I may know thee, that I may find grace in thy sight: and consider that this nation is thy people.

Ps. 5:8 Lead me, O LORD, in thy righteousness because of mine enemies; make thy way straight before my face.

Ps. 86:11 Teach me thy way, O LORD; I will walk in thy truth: unite my heart to fear thy name.

God has never kept His "way" hidden or obscured. God's "way" is available for all men to see and find. God has provided instructions in His "way", teaching men where they should go.

Ps. 32:8 I will instruct thee and teach thee in the way which thou shalt go: I will guide thee with mine eye.

Paul was a preacher of God's "way", a "way" that leads to salvation.

Acts 16:17 The same followed Paul and us, and cried, saying, These men are the servants of the most high God, which shew unto us the way of salvation.

The "way" of God is salvation. The destination of God's "way" is eternal life and bliss. We need to look to the Lord for this "way", we need to listen to His words as to this "way", for only through this "way" can man be saved. This "way" leads to victory, peace and life.

This "way" is through Jesus Christ.

John 14:6 Jesus saith unto him, I am the way, the truth, and the life: no man cometh unto the Father, but by me.

Jesus Christ is the "way". He is the One man must trust. Cain's "way" leads men astray. There is no other "way" to eternal life. The "way" of salvation is found in Christ.

Sadly, not many follow the "way" that God has provided. Some men travel down the "way" of the Lord but most follow the "way of Cain".

Rom. 3:12 They are all gone out of the way, they are together become unprofitable; there is none that doeth good, no, not one.

Prov. 14:12 There is a way which seemeth right unto a man, but the end thereof are the ways of death.

Men reject God's "way" and create another "way", a "way" after their own imaginations and foolish heart. To man, this other "way" seems better, superior, and grander than God's "way".

Men, through the knowledge of good and evil, have decided that there is a more excellent "way". This other "way" allows for the exaltation of the creature, man himself. Man can now be the focal point, the agent of reconciliation. Man will praise himself for his abilities in overcoming sin, Satan, and death. Man will be the hero in earning the grand prize of eternal life. Man will be his own savior.

Cain was the first to walk in this contrary "way". He cut the brush and left the trail for others to follow. He set out the lanterns and placed signposts along this "way". Therefore this ungodly "way" bares his name, "the way of Cain".

This path, walked by Cain, was originally narrow as he walked down it alone. His lone set of "footprints" was all that could be seen. When men began to multiply upon the face of the earth, they too sought this path. Fathers, mother, sons, and daughters have all walked this "way" of Cain. So many have walked Cain's path that it is now wide and well trodden.

Picture an original narrow path, only wide enough for one. As more walk down this path; this path begins to widen, eventually becoming a road so as to accommodate the many travelers. As more and more people travel this road, it is made wider and wider. Billions of people are journeying down this once narrow path. Christ calls this "way" "wide" and "broad".

Matt. 7:13-14   Enter ye in at the strait gate: for wide is the gate, and broad is the way, that leadeth to destruction, and many there be which go in thereat:
Because strait is the gate, and narrow is the way, which leadeth unto life, and few there be that find it.

The Lord tells us that Cain's "way" is "broad"; it has been expanded to accommodate all the traffic on the "way of Cain". So what was once a single person's path is now a wide expressway. The entrance gate is large. The signs along this "way" all read the same, "follow here to eternal life", as first etched by Cain.

The "way" of the Lord is not traveled as much as the "way of Cain". Consequently it is a narrow "way" by comparison, which only few have walked. It remains narrow and has not been widened by the flow of mankind. Just because the "way" of the Lord is narrow does not mean that it is hard to find or hard to follow. Christ is making reference to the fact that not many men travel His "way" as compared to Cain's "way".

The "way" of Cain leads to destruction and death, though the signs along it say otherwise. No peace, safety, and bliss will be entered into when the road reaches its end; only hell, fire, and damnation. Do not be swayed by the billions who travel his "way", do not be swept up by the flood of mankind as they hastily run toward their deaths. Admire not the tapestries, pageantry, and splendor of the "way of Cain". If those you know bid you to travel with them, run from them! Steer clear, look away, and be not deceived, for Cain's "way" will be to your destruction.

Ps. 119:101 I have refrained my feet from every evil way, that I might keep thy word.

Ps. 119:104 Through thy precepts I get understanding: therefore I hate every false way.

Prov. 4:19 The way of the wicked is as darkness: they know not at what they stumble.

Religious leaders stand in Cain's "way", directing traffic. They point to his "way", offering their services as guides for the masses to follow. Fortify yourself against these men, men who will only cause you hurt, men who brighten a path of death. Look to the Lord, for in Him will be found the true "way", the "way" to righteousness and eternal life.

Prov. 2:12 To deliver thee from the way of the evil man, from the man that speaketh froward things;

Prov. 15:9 The way of the wicked is an abomination unto the LORD: but he loveth him that followeth after righteousness.

There are only two "ways". One provided by God and a counterfeit "way" established by man. Each person chooses the "way" he will follow. God counsels man to journey down His "way", for only in His "way" will eternal life be granted.

Prov. 8:13 The fear of the LORD is to hate evil: pride, and arrogancy, and the evil way, and the froward mouth, do I hate.
Prov. 12:15 The way of a fool is right in his own eyes: but he that hearkeneth unto counsel is wise.

CHAPTER 14

THE WAY OF CAIN

All men want to live forever. From the day a man is born, he will toil and work for this one goal above all else. Death is a given; it begins the moment one is born. The only cure is eternal life, a life that does not end, a life free of death. It is to this end that men seek a "way", a "way" to have the victory over death and stand having obtained life eternal.

In this quest for eternal life there is one thing that is sought over and above all else, righteousness. For he who is declared righteous will be granted eternal life. Sin, death, and the Devil are all nullified by righteousness, for they are all silenced against one who is right. Sin will not have the power to stain you, the law will not be able to judge and condemn you, and the Devil will not be able to accuse you. Yes, righteousness does away with all of these. Righteousness is the key to unlocking eternal life; it provides the access and entrance to paradise. Therefore men seek to obtain righteousness. If one is righteous, he cannot be touched by condemnation and thereby excluded from eternal life.

Only two kinds of righteousness are available. One is God's and the other is man's. Man can only choose from these two.

Cain was the first to walk in a "way" that sought to establish man's own righteousness. Cain didn't want the righteousness offered by God.

Rom. 10:3 For they being ignorant of God's righteousness, and going about to establish their own righteousness, have not submitted themselves unto the righteousness of God.

70

Cain wanted righteousness apart from God, a righteousness that was independent of the Creator. He went about to establish his own righteousness. Thus Cain developed a "way" in which he could obtain this man-made righteousness.

This "way of Cain" is a way ordered by man's heart. This "way" seeks eternal life by man. Cain looked at himself and found a "good" through which he thought  he could gain eternal life. He looked at his own "good" and became charmed, enthralled, and obsessed with it. It was this "good" that Cain was to trust, believe, and stand in; just as his father Satan did when he fell from heaven. They were both corrupted because of pride.

Ezek. 28:17a Thine heart was lifted up because of thy beauty, thou hast corrupted thy wisdom by reason of thy brightness:

This "good" Cain declared was going to be his "way" to immortality. This "good" would overcome any sin or evil within him. This "good" was going to allow Cain to produce the righteousness that he needed to gain eternal life. Thus Cain established a "way" to walk after this "good", a "way" that leads to the praise of one's own goodness and self.

He believed that God would be forced to grant him eternal life because he deserved it because of his "good". Cain reasoned that God would be unjust in condemning a "good man". God could never refuse Cain's goodness, for Cain had determined that it was worthy and acceptable. It was this that Cain grasped and believed.

Cain ordered his steps to follow after his own "good". **Mankind has followed Cain in believing that men are good, that if given enough time they can clean themselves up and be fit for eternal glory.** This "way" dominates man's thinking today; reasoning that man is basically "good" and that God must accept him because of it. Man will be his own savior, because his own goodness will save him. Man can be made righteous by being "good".

The person who chooses to stand in his own righteousness must perform good works, establishing their self-righteousness. Men labor and toil in perfecting their works. They depend on their religious works; they take vows of piety, live humbly, give money, etc. trusting in these for salvation. New acts of worship are invented; pilgrimages, fastings, chants, baptisms, cutting of oneself, are performed in their desire for self-righteousness. A new cross is carried by these men; a cross whereby they sacrifice themselves for themselves. All this they do to be accepted and granted eternal life. To show just how much "good" they have.

Man looks to law-keeping as a way of self-righteousness. The law is used to compare themselves with each other. Man uses God's ten commandments as a measuring stick to determine how "good" he has been. The more the law is kept, the more the balances of judgment will tip their way. The purpose of God's law has been perverted and is now used as a "way" to provide man with his own righteousness.

Thus the "way of Cain" is man's attempt to conquer death, to remove the sting of sin and stand on the other side of this life victorious holding the cup of eternal life all apart from God.

The "way of Cain" leads men to be puffed up in their pride and self-righteousness. Men seek to conquer sin and death, to abolish them on their own. Professing themselves wise, they demand that a loving God would praise their "good". God would never punish and cast away a man who has tried his best to be "good".

Man has embraced this "way". This "way" has taken on many names and forms, but it is all the same "way". Call it what you will, give it all the names you want, but it is still the "way of Cain". All religions of the world are the same at their core; man's works can earn eternal life. Each religion may have a different set of markers by which men seek eternal life, but in the end they are all works-based. These works, though different in scope and grandeur, are works nonetheless. **This is the "way of Cain", a way of works, a way of declaring one righteous by his own strength, self-righteousness. Much of what goes under the name of Christianity is really the "way of Cain".**

All this stems from "the knowledge of good and evil". Man uses this knowledge to determine by himself what is "good" and what is "evil". Through the use of this knowledge man determines that he is "good", that he merits eternal life. Through this knowledge man declares himself righteous based on his own merits, works, and deeds. With this knowledge, Cain established "the way of Cain".

CHAPTER 15

GOD CONDEMNS THE "WAY OF CAIN"

The "way of Cain" is all about self-righteousness. What does God say about man's attempt to be righteous? Is man inherently "good"? Will God be forced to grant eternal life to those who stand in their own goodness? These are the questions we must ask God, our own reasoning and surmising are irrelevant and need to be discarded. It doesn't matter what man thinks and believes. Man is not the authority.

In the scriptures, we find God condemning man's efforts to make himself righteous. Beginning in Genesis, God states that the use of the knowledge of good and evil will cause all men to die.

Gen. 2:17   But of the tree of the knowledge of good and evil, thou shalt not eat of it: for in the day that thou eatest thereof thou shalt surely die.

The knowledge of good and evil brings death. This knowledge does not produce love, joy, peace, and eternal life. It produces the opposite: misery, hatred, corruption, and finally death. Man looks to this knowledge for life but God only sees death. We must believe the words of God and commit our own imaginations to the dung heap.

In spite of this truth, that the knowledge of good and evil brings death, man in his vain pride did not heed God. Man continued to insist that he could become righteous through his own works. Consequently, God continued to state many times over that man cannot overcome death, that man's righteousness would be of none effect.

74

Ps. 39:5b verily every man at his best state is altogether vanity. Selah.

Try as one may, be the best that you can be, but in the end man will be found wanting. The righteousness that one produces will be judged as vanity. "Every man", and that means all men, are included in the truth of this verse. No matter how hard you may try or how good you are, it will provide no benefit; it will be useless, unprofitable, and vain.

Ps. 62:9 Surely men of low degree are vanity, and men of high degree are a lie: to be laid in the balance, they are altogether lighter than vanity.

Your status in life is of no advantage in the eyes of the Lord. Whether you are at the bottom of society or at the top, all will be judged equally. All men will be placed in the balances and all will have the same result: vanity. Man's righteousness shall be valued as utterly useless and discarded.

Isa. 57:12 I will declare thy righteousness, and thy works; for they shall not profit thee.

Isa. 64:6 But we are all as an unclean thing, and all our righteousnesses are as filthy rags; and we all do fade as a leaf; and our iniquities, like the wind, have taken us away.

The righteousness that man builds, frames, and produces, God views as filthy rags. Rags that have no value and belong in the trash. This is true of "all" man's righteousness, not just some of it, but all of it. Bring to God everything you think is right and good; lay it before God; and it will all be judged as worthless. There is no man made righteousness that God will ever judge as being of value.

Rom. 3:23   For all have sinned, and come short of the glory of God;

The reason that man fails in achieving righteousness on his own is that all men are sinners. All men are born in sin, and commit sins. From one's grandma, to oneself, all are sinners. It is sin that prevents man from producing righteousness. Man's nature is totally corrupt. He is defiled and unclean. Each time one attempts to reach into heaven with one's goodness, they come up short. Therefore, one cannot be righteous in one's own strength.

God never says that man is inherently "good" or that there is a spark of goodness that men possess, but you will find these stated in the "way of Cain". The "good" that we think is in us is corrupted by sin; it is stained, warped, unable to produce righteousness. Man is not "good", man is a sinner whose nature has been ruined by the knowledge of good and evil. Do not be fooled into thinking that you are "good" as taught by the "way of Cain".

Paul pointed Felix toward God's "way" and away from Cain's "way".

Acts 24:22a   And when Felix heard these things, having more perfect knowledge of that way,

Acts 24:25   And as he reasoned of righteousness, temperance, and judgment to come, Felix trembled, and answered, Go thy way for this time; when I have a convenient season, I will call for thee.

Paul reasoned with Felix in regards to righteousness. Paul testifies to the truth that all men are sinners. Paul reasons for the truth, because the knowledge of good and evil resists this truth.

Rom. 3:9-10 What then? are we better than they? No, in no wise: for we have before proved both Jews and Gentiles, that they are all under sin;

The "way of Cain" turns men toward law-keeping to establish their own righteousness. They look to law-keeping for eternal life. Men believe that the law will be their ladder into heaven. But Paul reveals that the purpose of the law is not to bring man into heaven but to show man as a sinner.

Rom. 3:19-20 Now we know that what things soever the law saith, it saith to them who are under the law: that every mouth may be stopped, and all the world may become guilty before God.
Therefore by the deeds of the law there shall no flesh be justified in his sight: for by the law is the knowledge of sin.

Do not look to the law for righteousness. God declares that the law will not justify any man and will find every person guilty. All man's works, righteousness, good deeds, will avail nothing, for the law will declare all men guilty. **The purpose of the law is to show man that he is a sinner and that he cannot produce his own righteousness.** Guilt, judgment, death, and hell is what will be found by those who seek righteousness in the law.

Rom 3:10 As it is written, There is none righteous, no, not one:

No man will be able to stand in his own righteousness, and no man is "good" enough to enter heaven. Gather all the righteousness that you may; God will pronounce it vanity. Treasure it up to yourself, but it will still sink you into hell.

There are none righteous, not you, your spouse, sister, brother, or any one else you may know. Cain's "way" will not bring righteousness and life, but only condemnation and death.

Isa. 57:12   I will declare thy righteousness, and thy works; for they shall not profit thee.

CHAPTER 16

RIGHTEOUSNESS BY FAITH

There are only two kinds of righteousness, God's and man's. Knowing that God has condemned man's, we will now look to God's.

Dan. 9:7a O Lord, righteousness belongeth unto thee,

Yes, God is righteous, for righteousness belongs to Him alone. He holds righteousness and it is His possession. Search the heavens and only God will be found to have it.

Ps. 71:19 Thy righteousness also, O God, is very high, who hast done great things: O God, who is like unto thee!

God's righteousness is from above; it is not earthly. It is not born from the ground, not formed from the clay (man). His righteousness is much higher and purer than any we could produce. His is perfect.

Man needs God's righteousness, a righteousness that is perfect and unblemished; a righteousness that provides eternal life. Over the centuries men have looked to the Lord for His righteousness. Men such as Noah, David, Daniel, and Jeremiah knew they needed to look to God for His righteousness.

Ps. 31:1 To the chief Musician, A Psalm of David. In thee, O LORD, do I put my trust; let me never be ashamed: deliver me in thy righteousness.

Ps. 35:28 And my tongue shall speak of thy righteousness and of thy praise all the day long.

Jer. 23:6 In his days Judah shall be saved, and Israel shall dwell safely: and this is his name whereby he shall be called, THE LORD OUR RIGHTEOUSNESS.

But how can man gain this righteousness? Though seemingly as far from man as the east is from the west, God has made a "way". God, in His grace, has made it possible for man to have His righteousness.

Rom. 3: 21-22 But now the righteousness of God without the law is manifested, being witnessed by the law and the prophets;
Even the righteousness of God which is by faith of Jesus Christ unto all and upon all them that believe: for there is no difference:

Yes! God's righteousness is available to all men. A "way" has been made for all men to receive His righteousness and approach God. Men should praise God for being so kind and loving to His creation for providing His righteousness.

"But how," some may say? How can this be?

God in His grace sent His Son, Jesus Christ, as the "way". It is through God the Son that this righteousness is made available.

II Cor. 5:21 For he hath made him to be sin for us, who knew no sin; that we might be made the righteousness of God in him

Jesus Christ came into the world and took our sins upon Himself. He bore those sins on the cross and offered Himself a sacrifice. His sacrifice at Calvary was a result of His love for His creation. After making the payment for our sins, He rose from the dead.

The power of sin was so great that it took God Himself to deal with it. God could not leave this work to a created being; no angel, no archangel, nor man had the power to destroy sin. Why would God deal with sin in such a terrible and awful way as He did at Calvary, if there was another "way" such as promoted by Cain? If man could defeat sin in his own strength, then the cross (and the righteousness provided thereby) would not have been necessary.

Gal. 2:21 I do not frustrate the grace of God: for if righteousness come by the law, then Christ is dead in vain.

We needed God to fight this battle for us; we needed a Saviour to rescue us from the clenched fists of sin, death, and the Lake of Fire.

Christ conquered sin, hell, the Devil, and even death itself. Christ now sits at the right hand of the Father in heaven's glory as the conqueror of all of man's enemies. With victory in hand, Christ offers His righteousness as a free gift by His grace. He has taken your sin and offers you His righteousness.

Rom. 5:17 For if by one man's offence death reigned by one; much more they which receive abundance of grace and of the gift of righteousness shall reign in life by one, Jesus Christ.

Eph. 3:23 For by grace are ye saved through faith; and that not of yourselves: it is the gift of God:

God offers a gift of His righteousness that brings peace, joy, and eternal life. God desires to give us what we could never achieve on our own. What a wonderful gift, a gift that provides eternal life. How all sufficient is this gift, for man can rest from his vain works and receive this righteousness as a free gift of God.

Man only has to believe. Believe that the blood of Christ has paid for all of his sins. Believe Christ died on the cross for our sins and that He was buried and that He rose again the third day. When you believe, God grants you His righteousness.

Rom. 1:17 For therein is the righteousness of God revealed from faith to faith: as it is written, The just shall live by faith.

Rom. 3:28 Therefore we conclude that a man is justified by faith without the deeds of the law.

All men can have God's righteousness as their possession. God does not ask us to perform works for this gift. He does not want your money, your deeds, your works, or your "good". All of these are an abomination and can never earn you His righteousness.

In God's righteousness, the believer has conquered sin, the devil, hell and the Lake of Fire. He is translated from the kingdom of darkness and brought by loving arms into the kingdom of light. He is passed from death unto life through faith in Jesus Christ.

May we say with Paul:

Phil. 3:9 And be found in him, not having mine own righteousness, which is of the law, but that which is through the faith of Christ, the righteousness which is of God by faith:

Titus 3:5 Not by works of righteousness which we have

done, but according to his mercy he saved us, by the washing of regeneration, and renewing of the Holy Ghost;

CHAPTER 17

ABEL: A PROPHET'S OFFERING AND THE FAT THEREOF

Cain's true identity has now been revealed. He was a religious man, a Pharisee who believed the lie of Satan, his father. Cain was the first in the generation of Pharisees, the seed of the serpent. Let's return to the account in Genesis.

Gen. 4:3   And in process of time it came to pass, that Cain brought of the fruit of the ground an offering unto the LORD.

Gen. 4:4   And Abel, he also brought of the firstlings of his flock and of the fat thereof. And the LORD had respect unto Abel and to his offering:

Cain and Abel brought their offerings to the Lord; each brings something different. Abel's offering is accepted and Cain's rejected. There must be something significant about the offerings that they brought because God had respect unto Abel's and not unto Cain's.

Why did each bring a different offering and what effect did it have on the judgment of God? This is a very important question because there is much confusion and misunderstanding as to why God respected Abel's offering and not Cain's. Some feel sorry for Cain, believing him to be a victim of a whimsical God; consequently they accuse God of being unjust. This cannot be. We will look at this from the light provided by the scriptures and put to silence all those who accuse God of being unjust.

Let's first look at Abel's offering, which the Lord had

respect unto. It was by faith that Abel brought the proper sacrifice.

Heb. 11:4a   By faith Abel offered unto God a more excellent sacrifice than Cain,

And faith can only come by hearing the Word of God.

Rom. 10:17   So then faith cometh by hearing, and hearing by the word of God.

It was by faith in this word of God that Abel understood what to bring. Abel's actions were in direct response to commandments given by God. There was no room for misunderstanding; he didn't have to question what to bring or what to do. He knew. God had given His commandments in detail to both Cain and Abel. Abel by faith did according to what God commanded. Cain did not.

They had clear instructions from the Lord, instructions similar to those given by God to Moses some 1,600 years later. God's commandments to Abel instructed him to bring an animal, just as the law demanded years later. Abel did not bring just any animal (turtle, giraffe, lizard); he brought one from his flock, the same animal as the law was to require.

Lev. 1:2 Speak unto the children of Israel, and say unto them, If any man of you bring an offering unto the LORD, ye shall bring your offering of the cattle, even of the herd, and of the flock.

Abel also knew to bring the firstling of the flock. The Lord must have instructed him to do this. Abel did not randomly pick any animal from his flock. Abel's choice of the firstling of the flock coincides exactly with the requirements for an offering under the law of Moses. Abel's choice of the type of animal and that it be the firstling of the flock is in exact agreement with what the law was later to command. This did not happen by chance, Abel knew which animal from his flock to bring.

Num. 18:17 But the firstling of a cow, or the firstling of a sheep, or the firstling of a goat, thou shalt not redeem; they are holy: thou shalt sprinkle their blood upon the altar, and shalt burn their fat for an offering made by fire, for a sweet savour unto the LORD.

The similarities between what is commanded in the Law and what Abel does are not limited to the type of animal. When Abel brought his sacrifice, he knew what to do with it; he had to shed its blood. He knew the animal needed to be slain at the altar.

Lev. 1:5 And he shall kill the bullock before the LORD: and the priests, Aaron's sons, shall bring the blood, and sprinkle the blood round about upon the altar that is by the door of the tabernacle of the congregation.

Abel slayed the firstling of the flock at the altar just as the priests were to do under the law. Abel also knew to do something with the **"fat thereof"**.

Gen. 4:4a And Abel, he also brought of the firstlings of his flock and of the fat thereof.

Abel did not just slay the animal but he also offered the **"fat thereof"**. For Abel to offer the fat, he had to cut the sacrifice into pieces. He then laid the parts of the animal and the fat on the altar. This also is in agreement with what is stated in the law.

Lev. 1:12 And he shall cut it into his pieces, with his head

and his fat: and the priest shall lay them in order on the wood that is on the fire which is upon the altar:

It was no coincidence that Abel's actions agreed with what the law was going to require 1600 years later. The similarity between Abel's offering and what the law demanded can only have one explanation. **God must have provided the same instructions to Abel as given later to Moses.** God did not leave Abel to his own imagination as to what to do at the altar with his sacrifice.

Cain and Abel were given the same commandments, concerning the sacrifice, which Israel would eventually receive. God spoke to Cain and Abel not only about what kind of sacrifice to bring, but He also gave great detail in how to bring it, and what to do with it at the altar: a firstling from the flock, shed its blood, and offer the fat thereof.

Neither Cain nor Abel had any excuse for not offering the right sacrifice. Ignorance could not be claimed as a defense for rejection that day; they could not say that they did not know what to do. God had spoken. Both Cain and Abel were well aware of these instructions. **Cain was rebellious and disobedient to the clear commandments of God and Abel was not**. God was just in condemning Cain and for having respect unto Abel. This should answer any skeptic who condemns God and exonerates Cain.

Heb. 11:4a   By faith Abel offered unto God a more excellent sacrifice than Cain,

Abel by faith follows God's word. He did just what he was told. By faith Abel performs the works that were required in offering the sacrifice. Abel's faith is seen in the details of his offering, from the selection of the animal, to choosing the firstling of his flock, to the slaying of the animal, to the separating the sacrifice into its parts and fat. Abel did all this because he had faith in God's spoken word. Therefore Abel's faith is on display for all to see down through the corridors of time. Abel believed God and it was accounted unto him for righteousness.

Gen. 4:4b And the LORD had respect unto Abel and to his offering:

But how did God communicate His word to them? God many times used a prophet to speak His words. Could it be that God used a prophet to speak His commandments to Cain and Abel and if so who was God's prophet?

Jesus Christ again sheds further light on this in Luke. He states that the blood of a prophet was slain at the foundation of the world in Luke 11:51.

Luke 11:51-52 That the blood of all the prophets, which was shed from the foundation of the world, may be required of this generation;
From the blood of Abel unto the blood of Zacharias which perished between the altar and the temple: verily I say unto you, It shall be required of this generation.

The Lord says it was a prophet's blood that was shed from the foundation of the world; and then He says **"from the blood of Abel"**. Pharisees will be held responsible for **"the blood of all the prophets...From the blood of Abel unto the blood of Zacharias"**.

The Lord Jesus Christ identifies Abel as His prophet.

From Abel to Zacharias, the Lord Jesus Christ is including all prophets—from A to Z.

It was to Abel, God's prophet, that God gave the commandments about the sacrifice. A prophet is one to whom God speaks and in turn the prophets speaks to others. It was through Abel, God's prophet, that God spoke His word to Cain. This is how they knew what to do.

Cain didn't just kill another man when he slew Abel; he murdered the Lord's prophet.

Stephen, a man full of the Holy Ghost, condemns Israel, including the Pharisees.

Acts 7:52   which of the prophets have not your fathers persecuted? And they have slain them.

The "fathers" go all the way back to Cain, the first Pharisee who killed the first Prophet.

We have seen Jesus Christ make two references to Cain and Abel. In Matthew He identifies Cain as a Pharisee and now in Luke He identifies Abel as a prophet. Cain stood in his own righteousness and Abel in that of the Lord's. All of mankind is represented by one of these two brothers. Men are either attempting to placate God with their own works as Cain did, or they by faith trust in the word of God and receive God's righteousness. There is no other choice for men; all are either of Cain or of Abel.

CHAPTER 18

A WITNESS FOR ABEL

When Abel offered his sacrifice, he became a witness to the fact that he was declared righteous. Abel saw something happen at the altar whereby he knew that God accepted him.

Heb. 11:4a By faith Abel offered unto God a more excellent sacrifice than Cain, by which he obtained witness that he was righteous,

God did something in order to show Abel that he was accepted, **"he obtained witness that he was righteous"**. Abel did not have to question whether or not God was satisfied with his offering. God gave a witness to Abel about the acceptance of his sacrifice.

What was this testimony to which Abel was an eyewitness? Abel knew what kind of sacrifice to bring, he knew where to bring it, and he knew what to do with it. He knew to slay it, cut it into pieces, and lay it in order on the altar.

The last step in the offering of the sacrifice was to burn it with fire. A sacrifice was not complete without fire. The fire would consume the sacrifice and cause it to become a sweet smelling savour. The offering was only made complete by fire.

Lev. 1:9b and the priest shall burn all on the altar, to be a burnt sacrifice, an offering made by fire, of a sweet savour unto the LORD.

Lev. 1:13b and the priest shall bring it all, and burn it upon the altar: it is a burnt sacrifice, an offering made by

fire, of a sweet savour unto the LORD.

In scripture, God consistently used His fire, one that is supplied by Him, as a witness of His acceptance of an offering. God would send this fire from heaven to the altar on which the sacrifice had been laid.

When Elijah confronted the idol worshippers of Baal, they agree to offer sacrifices to their respective gods. They were to call upon their own god for fire. The one that answered by fire would be the true God.

I Kings 18:24 And call ye on the name of your gods, and I will call on the name of the LORD: and the God that answereth by fire, let him be God. And all the people answered and said, It is well spoken.

The Baal worshippers went first and they offered up their sacrifice, calling upon their gods to give witness through fire.

I Kings 18:29 And it came to pass, when midday was past, and they prophesied until the time of the offering of the evening sacrifice, that there was neither voice, nor any to answer, nor any that regarded.

After much pleading and crying, the Baal worshippers received no answer. No respect was shown unto their sacrifice. This resembles the scene with Cain. Cain laid his sacrifice on the altar and called upon God to give witness that it was accepted. Cain received the same answer: silence, no fire, no regard.

Elijah then offers his sacrifice; he slays the bullock, cuts into its pieces and lays it on the altar. Abel had performed the same actions when he offered his sacrifice.

I Kings 18:33 And he put the wood in order, and cut the bullock in pieces, and laid him on the wood, and said, Fill four barrels with water, and pour it on the burnt sacrifice, and on the wood.

I Kings 18:37-38   Hear me, O LORD, hear me, that this people may know that thou art the LORD God, and that thou hast turned their heart back again.
Then the fire of the LORD fell, and consumed the burnt sacrifice, and the wood, and the stones, and the dust, and licked up the water that was in the trench.

When Elijah prays to God, there is an answer. **God responded by sending fire from heaven to burn the sacrifice, to cause a sweet smelling savour.** God gave a testimony by fire, a witness that all could see with their eyes.

King David also received this witness by fire. David offered up to the Lord a sacrifice on the threshing floor of Ornan. With the sacrifice on the altar, David called on the Lord.

I Chronicles 21:26   And David built there an altar unto the LORD, and offered burnt offerings and peace offerings, and called upon the LORD; and he answered him from heaven by fire upon the altar of burnt offering.

The question must be asked: did David light a fire? And why would God send his own fire if David had already lit a fire? Could it be that David called upon God for His fire?

King David knew from the scriptures that God had His own fire, a fire that gave testimony to the acceptance of the offering. David looked for fire from God. Therefore he called upon God, much the same as Elijah did. **The Lord answered David by sending His fire from heaven.** It is important to note here that this fire came from God and not from the hand of David. The fire from God caused the sacrifice to become a sweet smelling savour and thus it was accepted. David received a witness, a testimony from God by fire.

The same happened with King Solomon. When the house of the Lord was finished, Solomon gathered all of Israel and offered a burnt offering. King Solomon does the same thing that his father did; he laid out the sacrifice and called upon God. He prayed to God. Solomon looked for a witness from God, testifying that what he had done was acceptable.

II Chronicles 7:1-3 Now when Solomon had made an end of praying, the fire came down from heaven, and consumed the burnt offering and the sacrifices; and the glory of the LORD filled the house.
And the priests could not enter into the house of the LORD, because the glory of the LORD had filled the LORD'S house.
And when all the children of Israel saw how the fire came down, and the glory of the LORD upon the house, they bowed themselves with their faces to the ground upon the pavement, and worshipped, and praised the LORD, saying, For he is good; for his mercy endureth for ever.

King Solomon knew that God had a special fire that was reserved for the altar and the offering. This fire needed to come from God and he could not substitute his own fire for it. This fire was a witness that God was pleased with the offerings.

When Elijah, David, and Solomon offered a sacrifice, they called upon God to show His acceptance. The sending of His fire showed God's acceptance. They knew that there was a unique fire that could only come from the Lord. God supplied this fire when the offerings were laid on the altar, a fire that gave witness.

Fire is found in the service of the Levitical priesthood. God gave instructions as to the duties of the priest. In these instructions God commands the priest to keep the fire of the altar going day and night. They were to never let it go out.

Lev. 6:9 Command Aaron and his sons, saying, This is the law of the burnt offering: It is the burnt offering, because of the burning upon the altar all night unto the morning, and the fire of the altar shall be burning in it.

Lev. 6:12-13 And the fire upon the altar shall be burning in it; it shall not be put out: and the priest shall burn wood on it every morning, and lay the burnt offering in order upon it; and he shall burn thereon the fat of the peace offerings.
The fire shall ever be burning upon the altar; it shall never go out.

The priests were to watch over this fire and make sure it was always burning. The priests were not to start a new fire with each sacrifice, but rather, keep the original fire going. There was something special about this fire, a fire that God wanted to burn continually.

This was a special fire. It had a unique origin, one that man was not to duplicate. When Moses set up the tabernacle, sacrifices were offered unto the Lord. It was at this time that the Lord sent a fire to the altar. The fire that was used for the altar came from God Himself. It was this fire from God that the priests were to keep continually burning, day and night. The fire for the sacrifice needed to come from God. Now it can be understood why the priests were to keep this fire going. It was God's fire, and man could not imitate it by starting his own fire.

Lev. 9:23-24   And Moses and Aaron went into the tabernacle of the congregation, and came out, and blessed the people: and the glory of the LORD appeared unto all the people.
And there came a fire out from before the LORD, and consumed upon the altar the burnt offering and the fat: which when all the people saw, they shouted, and fell on their faces.

The distinctiveness of God's fire, as opposed to man's fire, is seen by the two sons of Aaron.

Lev. 10:1   And Nadab and Abihu, the sons of Aaron, took either of them his censer, and put fire therein, and put incense thereon, and offered strange fire before the LORD, which he commanded them not.
Lev. 10:2   And there went out fire from the LORD, and devoured them, and they died before the LORD.

Nabad and Abihu bring incense unto the Lord, but they placed their own fire, fire that they had started, in the censer. **God calls this fire "strange fire".** This fire by Nabad and Abihu was man made; it did not originate with God. It was different in value. Man's fire was not the same as the fire that God sent. Man's fire was called **"strange fire"**.

The result of using strange fire was the destruction of both of these men. The true fire of God consumed them. The use of man made fire brought death; man was not to offer strange fire before God.

The censers that the priests used were to be filled with coals from God's fire at the altar.

Lev. 16:12-13   And he shall take a censer full of burning coals of fire from off the altar before the LORD, and his

hands full of sweet incense beaten small, and bring it within the vail:
And he shall put the incense upon the fire before the LORD, that the cloud of the incense may cover the mercy seat that is upon the testimony, that he die not:

The issue of fire is very important to God. God's fire was not to be replaced with man made or strange fire. This is because the fire represents the righteous judgment of God. With the sacrifice slain, the judgment of God is what falls on the sacrifice. God's judgment is seen in the form of fire. Man is not to usurp this judgment of God by using his own fire. Man's judgment is not the same as that of God's. It is God who is offended by sin, it is God's commandments that are transgressed; it must be God who judges. To offer strange fire replaces the judgment of God with that of man. Man is not God; man is not the one to judge. God's holiness is offended, and it is God's justice that punishes sin. The "way of Cain" seeks to overthrow God as the judge; this is the fruit of the tree of knowledge of good and evil, deciding what is acceptable. Who is the judge?

Fire is needed to show the passing of judgment upon the sacrifice. When the judgment and wrath of God fall upon the sacrifice, the sacrifice is consumed. If the judgment of God is satisfied, then it produces a sweet smelling savour, which is acceptable to God. The wrath of God against sin is passed; God's justice is appeased. The fire is symbolic of God's judgment, His wrath, His righteous anger against sin.

This judgment of God awaits all men, a judgment of fire against sin. Men should be in fear of this judgment, for it consumes and burns those subjected to the wrath of God. It was this judgment that Christ suffered when He went to the cross. God's judgment against sin fell on Jesus Christ. As Christ walked in the garden of Gethsemane, He sweat great drops as it were of blood, knowing the terror of God's judgment. Men today should be equally terrified of the judgment of God. They should be sweating, as did Christ, fearful to fall into the hands of a living God.

Jesus Christ offered Himself a sacrifice for our sins. He placed Himself on the altar, in our stead. He took our place, becoming sin for us, to bear the judgment of God. He bore the judgment of God against our sin, paying the price for our condemnation.

Eph. 5:2 And walk in love, as Christ also hath loved us, and hath given himself for us an offering and a sacrifice to God for a sweetsmelling savour.

As Christ bore our sins, the penalty and wrath of God was poured out upon Him. God's judgment, as typified by the fire, now fell on the Lord Jesus Christ as He hung on the cross. He satisfied the justice of God, becoming a sweet smelling savour. Payment for sin was made and accepted. Jesus Christ now offers this payment of sins to all men; He offers it as a gift, a gift that is to be accepted by faith.

Eph. 2:8 For by grace are ye saved through faith; and that not of yourselves: it is the gift of God:

Man can escape the fiery judgment of God through faith in Christ. Faith in Him alone saves us from the fire of God, without our works, without our strength or efforts. Man can either identify himself with Jesus Christ who bore the judgment of God as our sacrifice, or man can bear the judgment of God himself, eternally in the flames of the Lake of Fire.

In light of the foregoing study, concerning God's fire versus strange fire, we may have found the answer to our question.

The question being, "What did Abel witness at the altar that showed that God had respect unto his offering?"

Abel witnessed God's fire fall from heaven and consume his sacrifice. By this fire Abel gained a testimony from God that his sacrifice was accepted and he was righteous.

Cain, on the other hand, just like the Baal worshippers, received no witness, nothing happened, no fire from heaven.

In the end times Satan will counterfeit God's holy fire. He will cause fire to fall down from heaven above as a sign. This false fire of Satan will be used as a witness that he is the true God.

Rev. 13:13-14 And he doeth great wonders, so that he maketh fire come down from heaven on the earth in the sight of men,
And deceiveth them that dwell on the earth by the means of those miracles which he had power to do in the sight of the beast; saying to them that dwell on the earth, that they should make an image to the beast, which had the wound by a sword, and did live.

It is important not to confuse God's fire and Satan's fire, "strange fire".

CHAPTER 19

CAIN'S SACRIFICE OF "GOOD"

Cain brought a different offering than Abel. He did not bring an animal; he did not slay and apply the blood, he did not offer the fat thereof. **Instead, we see Cain standing there with a fruit basket.** Fruit that he had grown, something that he chose to bring unto the Lord.

Cain's fruit offering was not brought out of ignorance. As we have seen, he had the same instructions as Abel. He knew what God had commanded. Cain's fruit offering is a sign of an unthankful, unbelieving, and rebellious heart.

God had given His word for man to believe. Cain did not trust in God's word. Cain did not value the words of God; Cain did not obey God. He instead offered what he chose. This was in direct disobedience and open rebellion to God's commandments.

Upon rejecting the word of God, Cain embarked upon a different "way", a "way" outside of God's word. He sought to be declared righteous outside of the blood sacrifice. He imagined a new "way", a "way" to be declared righteous based on what he could do. Cain's fruit offering bares witness to this other "way", a "way" glorifying his own goodness and righteousness.

Cain declared that God must accept what he decided to bring. Cain was not going to be told what to do; he was not going to be obedient to the Lord. Cain followed his heart, a heart given to the knowledge of good and evil. Cain was going to be lord, ruler, and judge. He was going to be god. Therefore, Cain brought an offering contrary to God's word, born out of his rebellious heart. **He brought fruit, the fruit of his works just as unbelieving men still do today.**

The scripture doesn't reveal whether or not Cain approached the altar in religious apparel (long robe, miter, scepter, clerical collar, etc…), but if he didn't, it didn't take him very long to introduce religious dress into his "way". **The Lord Jesus Christ condemned Cain's men, the Scribes and Pharisees, for their false appearance of godliness.** Pharisees still dress according to Cain's "way".

Luke 20:46a Beware of the scribes, which desire to walk in long robes,

Mark 12:38a And he said unto them in his doctrine, Beware of the scribes, which love to go in long clothing,

CHAPTER 20

THE JUDGMENT OF GOD

The Lord judges the two offerings. God judges man by looking at the heart and searching it.

Heb. 4:12-13   For the word of God is quick, and powerful, and sharper than any two edged sword, piercing even to the dividing asunder of soul and spirit, and of the joints and marrow, and is a discerner of the thoughts and intents of the heart.
Neither is there any creature that is not manifest in his sight: but all things are naked and opened unto the eyes of him with whom we have to do.

It was at the altar where God searched the hearts of these two men. In Abel, God found the one thing He looked for, and that was faith. Abel heard the word of God and believed it. Because of God's word faith grew in Abel, faith that filled his heart, faith that caused him to use the members of his body to bring what the Lord had requested. This is what the Lord saw when He looked into the heart of Abel, a heart with faith in His word.

As the Lord passed judgment on Abel, He found a man of faith. Because of this, the Lord had respect unto the offering of Abel, for a heart of faith brought it. The Lord saw Abel's faith and declared him righteous. Abel is passed from death unto life. His sins are forgiven and the judgment of death against him is removed, and in its place God grants eternal life and peace.

Cain approached God after Abel. Cain was witness to the offering brought by Abel; he saw that the Lord had respect unto Abel's sacrifice. It was now Cain's turn to approach God. Cain placed his offering of fruit on the altar and looked to God to do the same for him, to declare him righteous, just as God had done unto his brother. God judged again, He judged the heart of Cain. God knew before He looked into Cain's heart that Cain came apart from faith because the fruit was evidence.

God looked into the heart of Cain looking for the same faith that He found in Abel. But instead of faith, the Lord found rebellion and pride. The word of God was not found in Cain's heart, it had been rejected and in its place was the word of Cain. Where God's word should have reigned, sat another word that ruled in its stead. God saw that the word of Cain usurped His own word. The word of God was cast out, not believed, and rejected. Rebellion against God and His authority had filled the heart of Cain. Cain would not be obedient to the word of God, the same word of God that Abel was obedient to. Cain mutinied against God's authority.

The Lord found in Cain a heart full of self-righteousness, a heart relying on himself to be his own savior. Cain was his own god, just as men are today.

In rejecting God's commandments, Cain was saying "God, I will decide what to offer. You must take what I want to give!" Cain had the boldness to challenge God's authority. Only a heart filled with pride would do such a thing. **The "way of Cain" gives commandments and orders to God.** It tells God what to do. Placing God as a servant, the "way of Cain" barks its decrees as the master. This is still how the "way of Cain" operates today. **Religious men dictate to God what He must accept or reject, they tell God what is good and what is evil.**

Cain was filled with self-righteousness, he had determined

that his own good works (as personified in his good fruit) were enough to cover any sin, and thereby he was just in his own sight. He had no need of a blood sacrifice for his sins, for he had proven himself righteous and holy by his own works. Cain looked not for God's righteousness, but for God's praise on how good he was. God found Cain's heart to be corrupted by the knowledge of good and evil, a heart beating with self-righteousness, and a soul that was clinging to this knowledge.

God's response to Cain was silence. There was no acceptance of Cain's fruit; there was no granting of righteousness, nor blessing to Cain. The judgment of death that was pronounced on mankind still hung over Cain. Cain had come to God in a state of spiritual death and God could do nothing but leave him in that state. The silence of God testified to His rejection of the fruit that Cain had offered. There was no praise from God, there was no shout of joy over Cain's good works; there was only the deafening silence.

CHAPTER 21

THE WRATH OF CAIN

Cain saw his brother accepted and declared righteous by God. But to Cain there was only rejection of his beloved fruit. This was supposed to be the big day, the day where Cain would be magnified before all his family. This was to be his defining moment when God would praise Cain as the promised seed. Cain had invested much time in preparation; readying himself for this grand day of his exaltation. This day was to be Cain's joyous re-entry into the garden, a day in which he would set everything right. Consequently when his expectations weren't met, he was angry.

Gen. 4:5 But unto Cain and to his offering he had not respect. And Cain was very wroth, and his countenance fell.

Cain finds himself standing alone, rejected by God, without respect, in front of his brother and probably his parents.[1] The heart of Cain now began to grow angry. Cain had put his trust in his own good works. **He couldn't believe that God would refuse him, a man who was holy and just in his own sight.** Cain's mind started to fill with rage at the

---

[1] It is in all probability that Adam and Eve where in attendance this day, watching their children present themselves before God. Adam and Eve watched with hope in their hearts as Cain presented himself, for it was in this child that they thought the blessed seed would be. They saw the acceptance of the animal sacrifice by Abel, and now they see the silence of God toward Cain. What disappointment they had when they saw Cain bring his fruit and not the animal sacrifice as commanded. Their hearts must have dropped as they saw the rebellion of Cain. Maybe they pleaded with him to go back and bring the right sacrifice. All their hopes and dreams came to a crashing end as they witnessed their son reveal himself for who he always was, a hypocrite, an ungodly man.

thought that God did not accept his good fruit. "Who is this God that refuses me!" Cain began to think. The fury built and soon filled his body; he couldn't hide the tumult inside. His face began to contort, his lips shook and trembled, his teeth clenched with force. Every muscle tightened with fury against the God who refused to praise the goodness of Cain. The blackness that was present in his heart now manifested itself in a wrathful bodily posture. Cain's rejected pride now produced the fruit of rage and hatred against God.

Cain's anger was clear to see, the word "countenance" means the external appearance. Cain's whole bodily shape was being transformed by the anger that was inside. Cain had become so wrathful that he could not contain it, but now it was manifested for all to see. Cain becomes as a madman, shaking his fist at God, cursing and blaspheming Him. Cain's **"wroth"** was directed at God.

The same physical expressions of anger and wrath were seen in Nebuchadnezzar when three men did not praise the image he set up to himself.

Dan. 3:19a Then was Nebuchadnezzar full of fury, and the form of his visage was changed against Shadrach, Meshach, and Abednego:

Pride, when rejected, causes such rage and fury that it cannot be contained, but oozes out every pore of the body. Men lifted in pride may seem peaceful, loving, and kind but wait; reject their good works, refuse to say they are worthy of heavens glory, do not admit they are righteous and holy and then you will see their true nature. They will be transformed before your eyes. The smile on their face will be replaced with clenched teeth, their eyes will burn with fire, and their veins will protrude as they fill with a mixture of wrath and blood. Their hands will tremble and their legs shake as their true heart is seen for what it is. This they try and conceal, but when they are rejected, and their works denied, they cannot contain.

All of Cain's anger came from a man who made the claim that he was "good". How could this be if Cain was truly "good"? Yet the man who boasted of his own good works and righteousness now becomes a man overflowing with hatred and rage. The good fruit of Cain never did remove sin; but had caused more sin, more rebellion, more hatred toward God. Thus Cain's outward appearance is changed, changed by his good fruit into a man of rage and hatred toward God, displayed for all to see.

CHAPTER 22

GOD'S RESPONSE TO CAIN'S WRATH

Cain's reaction of wrath and rage against God was clearly evident for all to see. God was there, witnessing this assault by Cain. It was then, while Cain was spewing out his fury against God, that God speaks.

Gen. 4:6 And the LORD said unto Cain, Why art thou wroth? and why is thy countenance fallen?

When the Lord decided to speak, He spoke directly to Cain in a very kind and affectionate way. God approached Cain with gentleness and love, with the hope of guiding Cain to a right standing before Him. The Lord did not take offense to the outrage of Cain; He did not respond with wrath and anger toward Cain. God could have easily destroyed Cain right there on the spot because of Cain's rebellion and rage against the Creator. Cain deserved to feel the full force of God's justice, striking Cain dead and sending him into eternal fire and torment. But God did not respond in this way. Instead God was patient and suffered this outburst by Cain. He now attempted to help Cain, to show Cain his error and futility of resting in his own works.

God's graciousness is evident; God is not quick to destroy the wicked but is willing to reason with the sinner.

Ezek. 33 :11 Say unto them, As I live, saith the Lord GOD, I have no pleasure in the death of the wicked; but that the wicked turn from his way and live: turn ye, turn ye from your evil ways; for why will ye die, O house of Israel?

Isa. 1:18 Come now, and let us reason together, saith the LORD: though your sins be as scarlet, they shall be as white as snow; though they be red like crimson, they shall be as wool.

He is longsuffering and patient. God is a great and merciful God who gives man opportunity to repent and accept His salvation. God began to reason with Cain as to the true nature of the problem, with the hope that Cain would repent from the "way of Cain".

God began by questioning Cain as to his anger. **"Why art thou wroth?"** The Lord was showing Cain that there was no need for this outburst; there was no need for anger. God asked Cain, **"Why?"** Why all the wrath? Why all the rage? Why all the cursing and bitterness?

This first question was intended to help calm Cain, to bring him back to a reasonable state. It is impossible to reason with someone when they are shouting and in a fit. They must first regain control of their emotions and then the mind can reason. This is what God was attempting to do with Cain, to calm him down so that he could be reasoned with.

God told Cain that his countenance had fallen. Earlier Cain was expectant and glad, but now he is not.

From God's perspective, this was to be a wonderful day for Cain. A day of salvation from the curse of sin, a day where Cain could once again have fellowship restored and be declared just and holy in God's presence. God was to deliver Cain from the bondage of death and sin and into a righteous standing before Him. Yes, this was to be a day of gladness and rejoicing, a day of thanksgiving to God for His wonderful grace.

The Lord now focuses Cain on the real issue.

Gen. 4:7 If thou doest well, shalt thou not be accepted? and if thou doest not well, sin lieth at the door. And unto thee shall be his desire, and thou shalt rule over him.

God again uses a question to cause Cain to think about what has happened. These questions were intended to bring about reasoning in Cain and aid him in recovering himself from his great error.

God stated that if Cain had done well, he of course would have been accepted. God is a just God and His judgments are true and right. God would not reject a righteous man or condemn an innocent man. Paul writes about the justice of God and His judgments.

Rom. 2:2 But we are sure that the judgment of God is according to truth against them which commit such things.

God's judgments are always according to truth; God is not a respecter of persons. His judgments are always pure and based on truth.

The Apostle Paul goes on to write how God will judge men. Paul opens the Judge's chambers and reveals the decision-making processes of the Lord God the Judge.

Rom. 2:6-8 Who will render to every man according to his deeds:
To them who by patient continuance in well doing seek for glory and honour and immortality, eternal life:
But unto them that are contentious, and do not obey the truth, but obey unrighteousness, indignation and wrath,

God will judge all men. Man will receive the just reward for his deeds. Paul makes it clear that if man can continually do well, then God will grant eternal life. God will not punish a man if he has continued every moment of his life to do well. If a man can be perfect continually, then God must and will grant immortality. But men are not perfect. We do not have the strength to do well every moment. We sin. Therefore God can never grant eternal life to those who trust in their "good', for all men fail at some point or another, all men sin.

Cain needed to realize that God was just in rejecting him. If Cain had done well, God would have honored him, for that would have been just. But God's rejection of Cain meant that Cain had not done well. **This is what Cain needed to understand, that despite all his efforts to produce his own righteousness, he couldn't do it.** And because of this, God was just in not accepting him.

CHAPTER 23

SIN LIETH AT THE DOOR

God instructed Cain as to the reason He did not have respect unto his offering. The answer was sin. The Lord makes this clear when He says, **"sin lieth at the door"**. This door, as shall be discussed in a later chapter, is a reference to the entry point of heaven. Cain cannot enter in because sin is preventing him.

This is a powerful point that the Lord made, and one that all men should be well acquainted with. Men are sinners by nature, and no matter how hard they try in their own strength to deal with sin, they still fall victim to its deadly grasp. Man does not have the strength to overcome sin or to make oneself fit for immortality. Men cannot live perfect lives, thus God is righteous when He rejects men on the basis of their own works.

The imagery of sin lying at the door can be likened to a dog that lies in front of a door. When anyone approaches the door, the dog rises with fangs bare, blocking the way. No matter how carefully one may try to go through the door, the dog will always be denying entry. The door cannot be accessed without first dealing with the dog. Every time man approaches the door, sin will be there preventing entrance. Man's problem is sin; sin keeps us at bay from the house of God.

The phrase **"sin lieth at the door"** has two meanings. The first has to do with the fact that sin is in the way of the door, forbidding entrance. The second refers to the fact that there is a sin offering at the door. A sin offering that bore man's sins, allowing entrance.

God has provided a sacrificial lamb that has become our sin, and now the Lamb of God is at the door. The dog, representing man's sin, can be replaced with God's sacrificial Lamb.

This can be seen clearly in the law that was given to Israel. Upon the day of the burnt offering, a man would approach as a sinner and place his hand on the animal's head. He thus identified his sins with the sacrifice, the animal and his sins became one. The sacrifice bore the sins of the sinner. The animal that carried the sin of the man was slain before the door of the tabernacle. Thus before the door of the tabernacle there was the man's sin and the animal sacrifice, both together, the two had become one.

Lev. 1:4 And he shall put his hand upon the head of the burnt offering; and it shall be accepted for him to make atonement for him.
Lev. 1:5 And he shall kill the bullock before the LORD: and the priests, Aaron's sons, shall bring the blood, and sprinkle the blood round about upon the altar that is by the door of the tabernacle of the congregation.

The law, with all of its types and pictures, has its fulfillment in Christ. When Christ left heavens glory to die on the cross, Christ was made our sacrifice.

Eph. 5:2 And walk in love, as Christ also hath loved us, and hath given himself for us an offering and a sacrifice to God for a sweetsmelling savour.

When Christ offered himself to be our sacrifice, He became sin for us.

2 Cor. 5:21 For he hath made him to be sin for us, who knew no sin; that we might be made the righteousness of

God in him

Christ becoming sin for us shows how sin can lie before the door, and at the same time, shows how there is an acceptable sacrifice before the door. Christ became both, sin and a sacrifice. How beautifully God weaves the stitching of this sacrifice throughout the whole Bible, all culminating in Jesus Christ our Lord.

This is the question that all men should ask: What are you going to do about your sin that lieth before the door? Are you going to try and remove it yourself as did Cain, or are you going to identify yourself with Jesus Christ through faith in His sacrifice for you? The "way of Cain" has you standing before the door in your sins. The "way" of God has you standing in the Sacrifice (Christ) that God provides before the door. No matter what, sin does lie at the door. It either bars the way, or it points to the Sacrifice that has been made sin. If one trusts in God's Sacrifice, the door is open for men to freely enter. The choice is yours; entry through the door will depend on how you deal with sin.

The Lord is patient with Cain. He reasons with Cain, attempting to draw him from his own destructive "way". God is longsuffering as He provides Cain with time to bring the right sacrifice. The Lord told Cain that his sin was barring the way, but that there was a sin offering for him at the door, and he could offer it as Abel had. Through the blood of the proper sacrifice, sin could be dealt with appropriately, and Cain could be accepted. Our God is a gracious and kind God, even to his enemies, such as Cain.

Rom. 5:10 For if, when we were enemies, we were reconciled to God by the death of his Son, much more, being reconciled, we shall be saved by his life.

Cain could have been saved that day, he could have listened to God's words and returned to the altar with the proper sacrifice, one such as Abel's. Yes, Cain should have fallen on his face before the Lord and thanked God for the great mercy that was shown to him that day. But Cain did not.

Gen. 4:7b And unto thee shall be his desire, and thou shalt rule over him.

The last issue that the Lord addresses with Cain is in regard to his standing with his brother. Cain wanted the preeminence over his brother; he thought the blessings of the promised seed should be his because of his birthright. Cain was born first, and usually the blessings of the father were to the firstborn. Cain yearned for this blessing. He thought it should be his.

Cain could have stood at the forefront of God's seed line, but he refused to approach God by faith. God offered Cain a chance to have that position, but Cain needed to have faith in the word of God and bring the right offering. With faith Cain would have ruled over Abel, for he would had been the promised seed. But Cain would not place his faith in God. He rejected God's word and therefore the blessing of the promised seed passed to Abel, who did have faith.

CHAPTER 24

THE DOOR

Gen. 4:7a If thou doest well, shalt thou not be accepted? and if thou doest not well, sin lieth at the door.

God referenced a door when He rebuked Cain. Sin lies at the foot of this door.

The meaning of the term "sin lieth" has already been discussed. It was shown to have two meanings. The first shows that man's sin is barring the door, preventing entry. The second identified a sacrifice that has become sin at the door. But what exactly is this door?

When the sacrifice was brought under the Levitical priesthood, it was placed on the altar. The position or placement of this altar is important as it relates to the meaning of the door.

Lev. 1:3 If his offering be a burnt sacrifice of the herd, let him offer a male without blemish: he shall offer it of his own voluntary will at the door of the tabernacle of the congregation before the LORD.

Lev. 1:5 And he shall kill the bullock before the LORD: and the priests, Aaron's sons, shall bring the blood, and sprinkle the blood round about upon the altar that is by the door of the tabernacle of the congregation.

The altar was in front of the door of the tabernacle. The sacrifice was to be made at this place, before this door. The door was the entrance into the tabernacle and the altar was in front of the door.

Lev. 4:7 And the priest shall put some of the blood upon the horns of the altar of sweet incense before the LORD, which is in the tabernacle of the congregation; and shall pour all the blood of the bullock at the bottom of the altar of the burnt offering, which is at the door of the tabernacle of the congregation.

Lev. 4:18 And he shall put some of the blood upon the horns of the altar which is before the LORD, that is in the tabernacle of the congregation, and shall pour out all the blood at the bottom of the altar of the burnt offering, which is at the door of the tabernacle of the congregation.

God dwelt in the tabernacle. He took residence there, filling it with His glory. There was only one way into the tabernacle; it was through this door. Therefore, God and man meet at the door, with the altar between them.

Ex. 29:42 This shall be a continual burnt offering throughout your generations at the door of the tabernacle of the congregation before the LORD: where I will meet you, to speak there unto thee.

Ex. 33:7 And Moses took the tabernacle, and pitched it without the camp, afar off from the camp, and called it the Tabernacle of the congregation. And it came to pass, that every one which sought the LORD went out unto the tabernacle of the congregation, which was without the camp.

This door is the entrance into the abode of God. It is the way into His presence. **God allowed access to Himself through this door.**

It is before this door that man placed his offering on the altar. The Lord judged the sacrifice at this door, with His fire.

James calls attention to the fact that there is a judge who stands at this door.

James 5:7 Grudge not one against another, brethren, lest ye be condemned: behold, the judge standeth before the door.

It is God that stands before this door, to judge who may enter and who may not. It is God who judges the sacrifice for sins. The Lord Jesus Christ is the Judge at this door. He is the One who will judge all things. Man is not this Judge.

John 5:22 For the Father judgeth no man, but hath committed all judgment unto the Son:

Acts 10:42 And he commanded us to preach unto the people, and to testify that it is he which was ordained of God to be the Judge of quick and dead.

The "way of Cain" seeks to usurp God's authority in deciding what is good and evil. Cain places man behind the altar accepting or rejecting the sacrifice. Man puts on the judicial robe and becomes the judge. The verdicts that men pronounce–verdicts on sin, life, and heaven are all according to the "way of Cain", not the "way" of God. They are all made by false judges, judges with no authority.

The Lord Jesus Christ not only stands as Judge, but scripture also describes Him as the Door itself. The entrance into God's abode is through this Door, Jesus Christ. If you want to come unto the Father you must go through the Son, who is the Door.

John 10:7 Then said Jesus unto them again, Verily, verily, I say unto you, I am the door of the sheep.

John 10:9 I am the door: by me if any man enter in, he shall be saved, and shall go in and out, and find pasture.

The Door is all-important to God. He only has one Door and the Door is His Son. There is no other Door.

The "way of Cain" offers another door. This door stands opposed to the Door of God. When men seek to enter heaven they can chose one of these two doors.

Cain's door takes on many names such as self-righteousness, good works, religion, law- keeping, humility, repentance, sorrow for sin, donations, confession, and the list goes on and on. It is as long as the "way of Cain" can imagine it to be. Rather than Jesus Christ being the Door, Cain's "way" labels his door after false gods like Allah, Buddha, Astor, Janus, Ra, Zeus, Vishnu, Baal, or any other who claim to be God. These are all false doors; doors inspired by the "way of Cain", doors that lead to the Lake of Fire rather than to heaven.

God has only one Door, Jesus Christ. How beautifully God threads His Door throughout scripture. He is the One all must go through to enter into God's kingdom. He is the One who stands and judges, He is the One who offers Himself as a sweet smelling sacrifice, He is the One who is the "way". Therefore Christ can say:

John 14:6 Jesus saith unto him, I am the way, the truth, and the life: no man cometh unto the Father, but by me.

The picture is complete, Jesus Christ is the Sacrifice, He is the Judge, and He is the Door. Jesus Christ is everything. God's "way" is through faith in the sacrifice of His Son. When faith is placed in Jesus Christ, man is passed from death unto life and the door of Heaven opens allowing entry. This is the only way into the abode of God, through the blood of Jesus Christ.

CHAPTER 25

CAIN THE FIRST THIEF

If a man was to offer his sacrifice at a place other than the door of the tabernacle, that man was to be cut off.

Lev. 17:9 And bringeth it not unto the door of the tabernacle of the congregation, to offer it unto the LORD; even that man shall be cut off from among his people.

Bringing an offering to another door results in damnation. The "way of Cain" brings its fruit to another door that cannot give the blessings that come from going through God's Door.

There are those who attempt to gain entrance into heaven through Cain's door, attempting to bypass God's Door.

John 10:1 Verily, verily, I say unto you, He that entereth not by the door into the sheepfold, but climbeth up some other way, the same is a thief and a robber

There are men who try to climb into God's kingdom without going through the Door. They despise God's Door and refuse to go through it. They invent other ways to get around the Door. The Lord calls these men, thieves and robbers. They attempt to rob God of His glory!

Christ is not a robber or a thief because He is God. He does not need to take from God the Father because He is all that the Father is. Christ and the Father are One, being equal. Speaking about Jesus Christ, Paul says:

Phil. 2:6 Who, being in the form of God, thought it not robbery to be equal with God:

The "way of Cain" is a thieving and robbing system. One that makes man equal with God. This "way" takes from God and gives to man. Cain's "way" robs from God the ability to decide what is good and evil. It also attempts to steal His glory, and thieve eternal life.

Cain was a thief, attempting to rob God. He sought to climb in another "way", without the sacrifice that God commanded. Cain refused to go through God's Door; he left the altar and went a different "way". The "way of Cain" is a "way" that is populated by thieves and robbers.

Cain attempted to steal God's glory and take it for himself. He climbed a ladder of good works and religious zeal, in an effort to circumvent the Door and to enter another "way". The rungs of this ladder consisted of what man could do, good works. This ladder could not reach. Undeterred, Cain and his followers continue to erect their scaffolding. Their ladders are set on sand, and they don't have a solid footing, they surely fail and fall. God will judge them and cast them all into the Lake of Fire. Their ladders laden with their fair speeches and good works will go with them.

Jer. 7:9-11 Will ye steal, murder, and commit adultery, and swear falsely, and burn incense unto Baal, and walk after other gods whom ye know not;
And come and stand before me in this house, which is called by my name, and say, We are delivered to do all these abominations?
Is this house, which is called by my name, become a den of robbers in your eyes? Behold, even I have seen it, saith the LORD.

Jeremiah warns Israel that their house of worship was becoming a den of robbers. The priests left worshipping God and turned to idols. It was religious men who were turning the house of God into a den of thieves, robbing God with their self-righteousness and vain imaginations. Jeremiah warns Israel that it was the thieving priests who were corrupting the temple. This is Cain's "way".

Jesus Christ states that Israel's corrupt religious leaders had totally corrupted the temple, making it a den of thieves. These were Pharisees stealing from God.

Matt. 21:13 And said unto them, It is written, My house shall be called the house of prayer; but ye have made it a den of thieves.

God's house was completely infested with these religious wolves.

Jesus Christ calls the Pharisees, **"thieves"**, for they attempt to rob Christ of His glory, they attempt to climb into heaven another "way", to substitute the Sacrifice and pilfer eternal life from God.

There is no other "way" but through Jesus Christ. You cannot steal from God as preached by the "way of Cain". For God offers eternal life as a gift. The gift of eternal life is ours by coming to the Door and accepting it by faith. Only a fool would follow Cain through his door.

CHAPTER 26

THE KILLING OF ABEL

Cain rejected the word of God, the same word of God that Abel believed. Cain thought himself to be his own savior. When Cain's offering was rejected he grew angry with God. In spite of Cain's anger, God was gracious with Cain and offered him another opportunity to be declared righteous.

Cain could have repented of his "way" and brought an animal as God had required, but he did not. Instead, Cain leaves the altar, without receiving God's righteousness and blessing. He did not allow himself to be corrected by God; he refused the reproof of the Lord. He was stubborn in his pride and would not submit to God's authority. Cain's heart was filled with hate toward God.

Cain believed that God was unjust and unworthy to rule over him. Cain would rule in God's place, Cain would judge what is good and what is evil. His "good" became his god, and this is what he worshipped. Therefore the knowledge of good and evil (as imparted by the tree of the knowledge of good and evil) had dominion in the heart of Cain. The fruit of this tree, working in the heart of Cain, produced the "way of Cain".

God was now Cain's adversary, an enemy that stood against his "good". "How dare God judge me unrighteous," echoed in the heart of Cain. With anger in his heart and clinging to his own goodness, Cain left the altar, never to return.

Gen. 4:8 And Cain talked with Abel his brother: and it came to pass, when they were in the field, that Cain rose up against Abel his brother, and slew him.

Cain talks with his brother Abel. Here we have God's prophet and a Pharisee talking together. **They clashed–as always occurs when godliness meets ungodliness, when God's righteousness confronts man's righteousness.** Abel loved the Lord and was faithful to His word, while Cain loved himself and his "way". They talked of both "ways", God's and Cain's, what would you expect this conversation to be about if not this. Cain was angry and offended to the core by what Abel said, just like he was with God. This led to murder, the killing of Abel.

Cain's heart was cemented in its "way", a "way" of self-righteousness. As Cain talked with his brother, he defended his self-righteousness. He attempted to convince Abel that there was good in him, and that his own works made him righteous. This is the work of a Pharisee.

Cain's conversation soon turned to God and how unjust God was in rejecting his righteousness. Cain believed that God was not just, but a hard and evil Lord, one who would not accept the "good" of Cain. Cain condemns God because God condemned him. Cain needed to prove that God was unjust in rejecting his good fruit. God must be damned, for how else could Cain justify God's judgment against him? Cain impugned the judgment of God. Cain destroyed the character of the Lord to save the good fruit that Cain worshipped. God was at fault; He was the one who could not bare that Cain was good, if not equal to God. This is the work of a Pharisee.

Cain attempted to convince Abel, to encourage Abel to leave God and turn to his "way" of good works and self-righteousness. Cain was proud of his "way" and sought to convert Abel to it. Cain was the first to try and convert others to his "way"; he was the first to proselytize. This is the work of a Pharisee.

Pharisees seek to win souls to their religious way; with fair speeches and cunning craftiness they attempt to draw men after themselves. Religious leaders today still follow Cain, looking for converts to praise the goodness of man, to rebel against God's word, to fight against the judgment of God. These are the works of Pharisees.

Abel's response was not what Cain had hoped for. Instead of claiming good works for salvation, Abel continued to have faith in God's word. Abel stood opposed to all that Cain believed. Abel knew that his own good works availed nothing with God; he could not earn his own salvation. This is the work of a faithful prophet.

Abel did not follow Cain down the "way" of religion and works. He did not praise the "good" of Cain; he did not worship at the altar of man's goodness and would not bow to the god of good works. Abel stood against the words of Cain. Cain's "way" was as refuse to Abel, to be left in the draught of the dunghill. Paul speaks of the value that he put on his own righteousness and good works when he was a Pharisee.

Phil. 3:8b and do count them but dung,

As a faithful prophet of God, Abel opposed and rebuked Cain's wisdom. It is a "way" that leads to banishment and eternal punishment from God. Abel would not eat of the fruit of Cain; a fruit that had corrupted his brother and now sought to corrupt him. Abel's lips would not taste Cain's bitter fruit. This is the work of a faithful prophet.

Abel defended the justice of God. He agreed with God's decision in rejecting Cain, for God was right. Abel maintained that God is holy and righteous, that God is the authority. This is the work of a prophet.

Cain continued with his rage when Abel rejected him. Cain viewed his brother now as an enemy to his "way" of good works. The good fruit of Cain could not stand to be judged wanting. It would not allow others to judge it unworthy. The same anger that Cain had toward God was now directed toward Abel. Cain's wrath simmered ever since God rejected his "way'. This simmering hate began to boil when Abel also showed no respect toward Cain's good fruit.

Even man's "good" is corrupt. Man's attempt to be self-righteous is impossible, for it is ruined by sin and God will not accept it. Our "good" is built upon a foundation of sin, it will always fail, and it will always bring death. **And as seen in Cain, his "good" brings death, the death of his brother.** The "good" in man will kill just the same as the "evil" in man.

Wrath and anger dwelt within the heart of Cain just as it does in the heart of every unbeliever. His wrath was not content to remain inactive or silent any longer. His wrath wanted to vent and his pride demanded vengeance. Cain looked for a "way" to satisfy his wrath and pride. A thought grew in his mind and it was the thought of murder. Yes, murder; the killing of Abel his brother would give Cain the release that he sought. His "good" would have the last word; it would have victory, for in the end it would kill his enemy. So Cain began to plan this deed, his "way" now turned to violence.

"And it came to pass…" this shows that there was time between their talk and the actual murder, time for Cain to plot his evil deed. This murder was premeditated, it was thought out before hand. It was not simply an act of violence committed on impulse while in a fit of rage. This is the work of a Pharisee.

Cain initially masked his wrath toward his brother; he hid it in the depths of his heart, he cloaked his murderous intentions. He did not openly display his hate but waited for a suitable time, a time when he could find Abel alone and unawares. Cain succeeded in concealing his wrath. For if there was any suspicion of murder, Adam or Eve may have tried to stop Cain or warn Abel, but they did not perceive the intents of Cain's heart. Abel is also deceived and does not fear for his life. If Abel were aware of the murderous plot against him, he surely would have run from Cain. Cain was sly and skillful in covering his true feelings; waiting for the most appropriate time to carry out his evil deed.

Cain the Pharisee is a picture of all hypocrites, who under the guise of godliness, kill unsuspecting faithful men. He is a type and figure of all Pharisees; they feign holiness but have murder in their hearts. They hunt down godly men and wait for a suitable time to pounce on them to destroy. When the environment is favorable to their evil desires they will kill, but when the environment and circumstances are not right and they do not have the freedom to kill, then they will demonstrate patience, exercising restraint while waiting for the times to change.

This was true of the Pharisees during the earthly ministry of Jesus Christ. The Pharisees would not publicly arrest Jesus Christ for fear of the Jews. They plotted and waited for an opportune time when their deed could be done in the dark of night. They learned this from the "way" of Cain. They knew Cain waited for an opportune time to kill Abel; they followed his example when going after Christ.

Gen. 4:8 And Cain talked with Abel his brother: and it came to pass, when they were in the field, that Cain rose up against Abel his brother, and slew him.

So Cain waited for the opportune time, a time when Adam

and Eve were not around, a time when Abel would be alone and unsuspecting. The time finally arrived for Cain to slay his brother. All was ready; the trap was set to spring. He met Abel in the field; they were alone, away from their parents. Abel was unsuspecting, for Cain had laid the perfect trap. Abel was caught unawares as Cain revealed his true heart's intentions. Cain's countenance changed once again, from the holy and loving brother to the monstrous killer that he truly was. His visage transformed, much like when he was wrathful against God.

The wrath in Cain's heart rushed to the surface. Cain rose over his brother. The time had come for Cain's "good" to take its revenge. Cain pounced on Abel as a lion upon its prey. Cain pummeled his brother again and again, with rage; he lifted his hands and thundered down on Abel. No plea of Abel could stay the anger of Cain. Abel's pleading for his life fell on deaf ears. Cain would not be stopped from his "way"; he would not give into his brother's cries for mercy. His heart was hardened and was not moved even as Abel's blood began to run down his clenched fists. Filled with hate and fueled by pride he continued until Abel's body fell limply to the ground, dead.

Gen. 4:11b which hath opened her mouth to receive thy brother's blood from thy hand;

We do not exactly know how Cain killed Abel; whether with a rock, club, bare hands, or with another device. We do know that it was through the hands of Cain that the blood of Abel was shed. Abel suffered a bloody death by Cain's hands that caused his blood to stain the earth. This killing was personal with Cain, and as any homicide detective will vouch, murders of this nature produce some of the most horrific and violent deaths imaginable. It is more than just the killing of the body, it has much to do with the joy that the killer gets in releasing his anger while torturing his dying victim. These killers will continue to stab, beat, bludgeon, over and over and over again, long after the person is dead. Cain may have let his imagination run wild and devised a most tortuous way for Abel to die as he savored every last drop of rage and hatred.

Over the centuries Pharisees[1] have continued Cain's bloody, torturous, murderous "way". Pharisees have used their imaginations to produce the worst possible forms of death for their victims. It was never their intention to just simply and quickly and mercifully kill those they hated and despised, but to make death as fearful, painful, and as prolonged as they could. A quick and easy death for their victim would not satisfy the hate in the hearts of these men. Torturous racks, whips, fire irons, spiked cages, used as lighted torches, crucified, cut in two, impaled, boiled, fed to animals, etc...all are examples of Cain's murderous, bloody "way". Pharisees, religious leaders proclaiming goodness and holiness do this; when their "good" is refused, watch out. This was all learned from Cain.

The cruelty of Cain's men is most evident in the death of the Lord Jesus Christ. The Pharisees, upon seizing the Lord Jesus Christ, could not wait to turn Him over to the Romans knowing that the Romans would put Christ to death in the most excruciating and torturous way. In their plot to have Rome find Christ guilty and worthy of death, the Pharisees lied and brought false witnesses to accuse the Lord. It was also the Pharisees who riled up the people and caused them to demand that the Romans crucify Christ.

With Christ delivered to the Romans, the guards blindfolded and beat Him. He was tied and whipped. The Roman whips

---

[1]See next chapter - War with God

had bits of bone and metal in the ends so that when they struck the victim, they would tear chunks of flesh from off the back. A crown of thorns was pushed into His head, embedding them deep into his scalp. His beard was violently pulled, ripping the hairs from His face. His blood ran down His head and from the gaping wounds inflicted by the whip. The Lord's face was beaten and ripped apart to such a degree that He could not be recognized. The scriptures state that Christ was marred beyond recognition and more than any other man.

Isa. 52:14 As many were astonied at thee; his visage was so marred more than any man, and his form more than the sons of men:

A purple robe was placed upon Him as they mocked and cruelly abused Him. The robe was later torn away reopening any scabs and inflicting more pain. He was given a heavy cross to carry as He was paraded through the streets of Jerusalem being taunted, mocked and verbally abused by the thousands. At Calvary, He was laid upon the cross and with a hammer, the Roman guards pounded spikes through His hands and feet. The cross was lifted and with a painful thud dropped into a hole. Christ now hung, suspended by the nails. In order to breath, Christ had to lift Himself by pushing on the spike in His feet and pulling on the spikes in His hands. The pain was excruciating and intensified with each and every breath. Crucifixion was a long, slow, extraordinarily painful, torturous, way of execution.

The Pharisees watched with approval and in great pride and joy as Christ was violently murdered. This is the bloody "way of Cain".

Cain stood back and viewed his brother's lifeless body lying on the ground. **Cain's "goodness" would not kill an animal**

for a sacrifice, but it would kill and shed his brother's blood. The life of his brother was sacrificed at the tree of the knowledge of good and evil at which Cain worshipped. Cain's god of good works had claimed its first victim. Millions more were to come from the hands of his faithful followers.

With the deed done, Cain buried or hid the body. He then proceeded to clean himself up, to wash the blood of Abel from his hands and vesture, to wipe the splattered blood of Abel from his face. Cain returns home and quietly goes about his business as if nothing happened. He gave no indication of what he had just done. He resumed his godly persona, his hypocrisy.

Cain was a man whose "way" of "good" did lead him to become a murderer. **For murder does not only come from "evil", but also from "good" when it has been refused.**

CHAPTER 27

WAR WITH GOD

Cain declared war on God. In its opening battle, Cain kills God's prophet, Abel. Cain could not reach into heaven and slay the Lord, so he does the next best thing, he sheds the blood of Abel, God's faithful servant. Abel was killed because he stood with God, against the works of the flesh. He was killed because Cain hated God.

John 15:18-19 If the world hate you, ye know that it hated me before it hated you.
If ye were of the world, the world would love his own: but because ye are not of the world, but I have chosen you out of the world, therefore the world hateth you.

It is obvious why the Pharisees killed the Lord Jesus Christ, they were attempting to complete what Cain started, to kill God. Jesus Christ was slain because He claimed to be God. They plotted and premeditated His death. The world's hatred of God was not satisfied with the crucifixion of the Lord Jesus Christ. It still seeks more blood, the blood of those who stand with God.

Cain's murder started a long and bloody history of persecution by the church of Cain against the true church of God. These followers of Cain are all about the destruction and annihilation of God's faithful. They attack and devour any and all who stand against their god of "good works". They have sought to extinguish the true knowledge of God and replace it with their own knowledge and wisdom. This persecution has continued from the beginning of time and it still exists today.

We who have faith in the blood of God are always under attack by those who profess good works.[1] In the name of good works and to save the tree of the knowledge of good and evil they follow Cain's bloody "way".

The suffering that Paul promises to godly believers started with Abel.

2 Tim. 3:12   Yea, and all that will live godly in Christ Jesus shall suffer persecution.

It was Cain, the first Pharisee who killed Abel. It was the Pharisees who incited the masses to crucify Christ; it was the religious leaders who riled up the people against Paul. It will be religious men, following the "way of Cain" who will seek to destroy the righteous.

---

[1] Saints, for the most part, in America have had a reprieve from physical persecution for the last 200 years or so. Religious men have not had the political power to fulfill their heart's desire for murder. This is not the case in the rest of the world. From Iran to Saudi Arabia, Russia, China, Thailand, North Korea, Chad, Somalia etc…Christians are persecuted and martyred on a daily basis.

CHAPTER 28

CAIN'S DEED REVEALED

Cain's murderous deed was done in secret. Cain made sure that Adam and Eve could not hear the screams of Abel as he was viciously killed. Abel's absence was soon noticed. If God asked Cain of the whereabouts of Abel, would it not be logical to think that Adam and Eve asked the same question before God did. And if so, Cain had to answer his parents with a lie. Adam and Eve may have even searched for their son, looking in the fields where he once tended his flocks.

And now God confronts Cain about Abel.

Gen. 4:9 And the LORD said unto Cain, Where is Abel thy brother? And he said, I know not: Am I my brother's keeper?

The Lord questioned Cain. Cain did not respond with tears of guilt or shame, but with a lie. His conscience was not bothering him. Cain did not confess his sin. Cain knew he had killed Abel, he knew where Abel's dead body lay, but he sought to keep his bloody murder concealed. Cain tried to appear guiltless; he kept up the masquerade of a righteous and just man.

Cain was nothing but a hypocrite, just like the Pharisees who follow him. He was a liar with no love for his fellow man. Cain's true heart was seen in his answer to God. He has no regard for his neighbor.

When He responded back to God, **"Am I my brother's keeper?"** Cain is admitting that he doesn't believe that he is his brother's keeper. Cain's response is representative of all those who pride themselves in the law. **The followers of Cain say they keep the law; yet they break the fundamental principal on which the law hangs, just as Cain did. They do not love their neighbor.**

Lev. 19:18 Thou shalt not avenge, nor bear any grudge against the children of thy people, but thou shalt love thy neighbour as thyself: I am the LORD.

Gal. 5:14 For all the law is fulfilled in one word, even in this; Thou shalt love thy neighbour as thyself.

Cain, in all of his self-righteousness, could not even keep the basis for the law. In all of his professed goodness, he was never able to love his brother. **The knowledge of good and evil does not lead man to love his neighbor, but to love oneself.**

Cain's remark is one of the most well known and quoted passage of scripture. The reason that all men easily quote this verse is because this is the attitude residing in the hearts of unsaved men. They only care about themselves.

CHAPTER 29

BLOOD THAT SPEAKS

Gen. 4:10   And he said, What hast thou done? the voice of thy brother's blood crieth unto me from the ground.

God would no longer be restrained, He thundered against Cain! God knew what Cain did; He saw Cain commit the murder and heard Cain lie about it.

Abel was supposed to be silenced in his death, no longer speaking against Cain's "way". But Cain was deceived; Abel did not cease to speak. He did not remain silent. Abel's blood spoke. Abel still existed; he could cry even in death, he knew what happened to him. Even though he was dead to this world, he spoke from another. Abel's physical body was eaten of worms, but his soul was not extinguished. His soul lives on, and speaks.

Heb. 11:4   By faith Abel offered unto God a more excellent sacrifice than Cain, by which he obtained witness that he was righteous, God testifying of his gifts: and by it he being dead yet speaketh.

Men do not cease to exist when they die. Abel cries for justice, **"he being dead yet speaketh".** He accuses Cain of his murder. Night and day, Abel persistently calls upon God for justice and vengeance for his murder. Abel continues to trust in God, even in death, trusting Him to exact punishment against his murderer. He looks to God for vengeance.

Abel's blood can only cry. It is powerless to do anything else, such as returning from the grave to avenge his death. His blood can only petition God and ask for justice.

Abel's cries reached heaven, all the way to the ears of God. God hears the cries of Abel, his righteous servant. God is not deaf to the plight of His servants.

Ps. 34:15 The eyes of the LORD are upon the righteous, and his ears are open unto their cry.

Many voices have been added to Abel's cry for justice. All those who have perished under the dominion of Cain's "way" also cry out. Every saint who has been killed by Cain's men cries unto God. These saints cry with Abel.

Rev. 6:9-10 And when he had opened the fifth seal, I saw under the altar the souls of them that were slain for the word of God, and for the testimony which they held: And they cried with a loud voice, saying, How long, O Lord, holy and true, dost thou not judge and avenge our blood on them that dwell on the earth?

The scriptures teach that there is another blood that speaks, a blood that can do more than Abel's.

Heb. 12:24 And to Jesus the mediator of the new covenant, and to the blood of sprinkling, that speaketh better things than that of Abel.

The blood of Jesus Christ also speaks, and speaks of better things than that of Abel's.

The blood of Jesus Christ was shed on the cross. When Christ went to the grave, He was not held captive like Abel, but overcame death. The blood of Christ has power, strength, and life. It has power to overcome death, strength to resurrect from the grave, and is able to grant life to those who trust in it. The blood of Christ is better than Abel's because it is God's blood.

Acts 20:28b the church of God, which he hath purchased with his own blood.

What the blood of Abel could not do, the blood of Christ was able to perform. Abel could not overcome sin, death, and the power of the Devil; but Christ does all these. He paid the penalty for sin, He defeated the enemy of death, and He conquered the Devil. Only through the blood of Christ will you find these victories and eternal life.

The blood of Christ speaks, it testifies to many wonderful blessings that flow from God to man. Let us listen to the scriptures as they reveal to us what the blood of Christ speaks.

The blood of Christ speaks of peace with God.

Col. 1:20 And, having made peace through the blood of his cross, by him to reconcile all things unto himself; by him, I say, whether they be things in earth, or things in heaven.

The blood of Christ speaks of justification.

Rom. 5:9 Much more then, being now justified by his blood, we shall be saved from wrath through him.

The blood of Christ speaks of redemption and the forgiveness of sins.

Eph. 1:7 In whom we have redemption through his blood, the forgiveness of sins, according to the riches of his grace;

The blood of Christ brings us near to God.

Eph. 2:13 But now in Christ Jesus ye who sometimes were far off are made nigh by the blood of Christ.

Our salvation is possible because of the blood of Jesus Christ. Only the blood of Jesus Christ has the power to pay for sin and to give forgiveness to mankind.

God offers man the blessings of what the blood of Christ speaks as a free gift, to be accepted by faith alone, without works. God does not want man's dead fruit; He does not want man's vain imaginations. He only asks that you trust in the blood of Jesus Christ, that you cease from your works and lay hold of this most precious gift of God. Lay your fruit aside and trust in the blood of Christ through faith. Abandon the "way of Cain". This is what the blood of Christ is speaking to you.

Rom. 3:25 Whom God hath set forth to be a propitiation through faith in his blood, to declare his righteousness for the remission of sins that are past, through the forbearance of God;

Rom. 3:28 Therefore we conclude that a man is justified by faith without the deeds of the law.

Rom. 4:5 But to him that worketh not, but believeth on him that justifieth the ungodly, his faith is counted for righteousness.

Let us have faith in His blood and not in our own. We preach the blood of Christ and what it speaks–forgiveness of sins, victory over death, and eternal life.

Heb. 12:24b that speaketh better things than that of Abel.

CHAPTER 30

CAIN'S PUNISHMENT

Gen. 4:11 And now art thou cursed from the earth, which hath opened her mouth to receive thy brother's blood from thy hand;

God convicts Cain of murder and Cain stands guilty before God. There is nothing that Cain can say, he is silent; his mouth has been stopped by the righteous judgment of God. God executes judgment against Cain.

God first curses Cain; he curses him from the earth. This curse involves the promised seed. Forevermore the seed that was promised to Eve would not be fulfilled in Cain or any of his descendents. Cain's branch was broken off and his children are forever excluded from the lineage of the promised seed.

When Adam sinned, God cursed the ground and not Adam. The reason was that Adam was needed to produce a seed that would lead to the promised deliverer, the Lord Jesus Christ. Adam was not cursed the same way Cain was.

Gen. 3:17 And unto Adam he said, Because thou hast hearkened unto the voice of thy wife, and hast eaten of the tree, of which I commanded thee, saying, Thou shalt not eat of it: cursed is the ground for thy sake; in sorrow shalt thou eat of it all the days of thy life;

God also cursed Cain's vocation. The earth, which was forced to drink the blood of Abel, would no longer yield its strength and vitality to Cain.

Gen. 4:12   When thou tillest the ground, it shall not henceforth yield unto thee her strength; a fugitive and a vagabond shalt thou be in the earth.

Cain was also sent into exile, to wander with no certain dwelling place. He was sent away from his home, away from his fields and crops, away from his parents. He was to be a wanderer in the earth.

As men began to multiply on the earth, they were to remember God's words and shun Cain, driving him away. Men should have feared Cain; they should have been on guard against him, for he was a murderer and an outcast by God. When he drew near to them, they were to force him back into the wilderness, back to isolation and separation from mankind.

Cain's "way" did not earn God's favor but God's wrath. **The goodness and self-righteousness held by men will only result in being cursed by God.** The "way of Cain" leads to eternal separation from God in the Lake of Fire. Man should abandon his works as quickly as he would let go of a hot coal in the palm of his hand.

Gen. 4:13   And Cain said unto the LORD, My punishment is greater than I can bear.

Gen. 4:14 Behold, thou hast driven me out this day from the face of the earth; and from thy face shall I be hid; and I shall be a fugitive and a vagabond in the earth; and it shall come to pass, that every one that findeth me shall slay me.

Cain didn't respond with words of remorse, he was not convicted of sin, he did not break down in tears over what he has done, he did not feel or demonstrate any guilt in the slaying of his brother. He had no empathy for his parents for the pain he caused them. Instead, Cain cried for himself, because of his punishment.

His pleas were for his benefit alone. He was distraught over how God's judgment would affect him. He complained bitterly that he couldn't bear the punishment. Cain did not show the same concern for Abel as when he pleaded for his own life. **Cain did not heed Abel's cries or show pity when Abel's blood flowed. But when it came to himself, he begged and complained fervently about his punishment.**

Cain did not want to die. He worried that in his wanderings men may seek to kill him. He feared that another son of Adam would seek to take his life. Cain was frightened by these thoughts, thoughts of being hunted and killed.

Cain, in all his pride and arrogance was in the end a coward and scared to die. He never had confidence in facing death. This is how it is with Cain's "way". It professes to have understanding and wisdom about life and death. It teaches that it knows the "way" to eternal life and victory over death. **But when it is tested, when it has to look death in the face, Cain's "way" provides no comfort or confidence.** The soul is frightened and quivers at death's door. All of man's goodness, his works, his self-righteousness will provide nothing on which to stand when death calls, and he knows it.

Many men who have preached good works for salvation tremble when it comes time to die. They have no true hope in which to trust. One must turn to God, for only God grants grace and peace. Only He provides comfort and hope in the time of death. Then we may say with Paul,

I Cor. 15:55-57 O death, where is thy sting? O grave, where is thy victory?
The sting of death is sin; and the strength of sin is the law.
But thanks be to God, which giveth us the victory through our Lord Jesus Christ.

Cain failed to conquer death, he could not break its bonds, he could not remove the poison from its sting; therefore he pleaded for life.

Gen. 4:15 And the LORD said unto him, Therefore whosoever slayeth Cain, vengeance shall be taken on him sevenfold. And the LORD set a mark upon Cain, lest any finding him should kill him.

In answer to Cain's pleas, God gave a warning, that if men kill as Cain had done, vengeance would be taken on them.

Cain is to be a living testimony to the failure of his "way". God accomplished this by putting a mark on Cain and then banishing him into the wilderness. This mark was to warn others of Cain, a mark to cause men to flee before Cain, a mark to declare the rejection of Cain's "way". **Cain's wisdom, self-righteousness, and "way" was marked as cursed by God.**

CHAPTER 31

CAIN'S CITY

Gen. 4:16-17 And Cain went out from the presence of the LORD, and dwelt in the land of Nod, on the east of Eden.
And Cain knew his wife; and she conceived, and bare Enoch: and he builded a city, and called the name of the city, after the name of his son, Enoch.

Marked and banished by God, Cain wandered toward the land of Nod. Cain's curse was to live a life of isolation and shame for the murder of his brother. Mankind was to avoid Cain and leave him to his own "way". God's warning against Cain was to be taught and obeyed by all the future children of Adam. God never rescinded this commandment, and all men were to obey it.

But this did not happen. As man's population on the earth grew, men rebelled against the commandment of God to leave Cain alone. They did not shun or cause Cain to flee when he approached. Men set their hearts against God and they refused to obey His commandment. They did not follow God's word. Cain was not viewed as an outcast, but as a friend.

Cain's punishment as a vagabond came to a quick end as mankind sought out the company of Cain. Cain was sought after and revered by men. They accepted him and welcomed him. Cain the vagabond was now Cain the leader of men.

Cain takes a wife and starts a family. God never intended for Cain to have offspring, he was to die alone, without children. But now Cain has a lineage, he becomes a father.

Soon there are so many people living with Cain that a city is built. Cain builds the first city. He is the chief architect, the master builder after which other cities will be patterned. Cain is its leader and head. He is the first to establish a society, to create a culture that is governed by his thoughts and "way". Cain now has an outlet through which he can rule and influence the lives of all men with his "way".

The men of this city have joined themselves to Cain and have rebelled against God. They are living lives that are in direct opposition to the will of God. They are ungodly men who have gone after the "way of Cain". Cain's city rises as a witness against God; A kingdom that will rival God's kingdom.

Gen 4:20-22 And Adah bare Jabal: he was the father of such as dwell in tents, and of such as have cattle.
And his brother's name was Jubal: he was the father of all such as handle the harp and organ.
And Zillah, she also bare Tubalcain, an instructer of every artificer in brass and iron: and the sister of Tubalcain was Naamah.

Civilization is born through the sons of Cain. The rise of the performing arts is seen as songs, music, and plays are soon heard and seen in Cain's civilization. Mining, refining, and transportation of raw metals develop. Artisans take metals, shape and form them. Blacksmiths and jewelers produce every imaginable object. Markets are created where men sell their wares. The city is alive and vibrant as men begin to fulfill their desires, the desires of Cain.

Cain provided a place where men could indulge all their fleshly imaginations. It was from this first city that Cain was able to have a most profound effect on mankind. For this city was founded on his "way" and bore his influence. **This city**

was an expression of Cain's rebellion against God. The foundations of this city still exist today; Cain's blueprint is still meticulously followed. All cultures are filled with Cain's thoughts, imaginations, and "way". Cain, as the wise master builder of the "way of Cain", laid the groundwork for all future societies to follow.

CHAPTER 32

ENOCH: THE WORLD RELIGION

Gen. 4: 17   And Cain knew his wife; and she conceived, and bare Enoch: and he builded a city, and called the name of the city, after the name of his son, Enoch.

Unto Cain was born Enoch, his firstborn. Cain names his city after his son. Enoch means "teacher" or "initiator". In this city, Cain teaches mankind his "way". Cain begins to initiate men into his idolatrous system of worship. This city will be the religious focal point of the world.

Through Enoch, Cain permeates society with his good fruit. He did this by instituting a religious system and appointing himself as the head. He is the first to establish himself as a type of the anti-christ. He becomes the first Pope, Imam, Dali Lama, Sheikh, Ayatollah, etc.

Cain's "way" of religious works is taught to his followers. Through Enoch, he passes the torch of good works, his "way". Schools of religion and places of worship begin to populate this growing community. Cain begins the process of instituting priesthoods, men who are knowledgeable in all that Cain spoke. Mankind is now immersed in the system of worship that Cain started, Cain's "way".

Cain cannot grow food from the ground because of the Lord's curse. He turns to his religious system as a means to provide for himself. He, as the great high priest, in all likelihood institutes a tithe for his services. He collects money for the building of temples and the ongoing needs of his religion. **Cain has now found a way to reap great riches; he does this through religion.** He is the first

Pharisee to live off the labors of others, demanding a price for his priestly functions. Others will grow his food, others will labor and toil for him. He soon learns that much profit can be made when dealing in the souls of men. **He starts the "religious industry".**

Profiting from religion has continued down through the centuries, with Cain's men taxing the masses for their own bellies. They rob and steal. They sell religious trinkets, beads, statues, blessings, indulgences, confessions, prayers, there is no end to what they will do for money. These are all schemes of Cain's "way". Today's religious thieves have learned well from Cain, they have had 6,000 years to learn how to effectively traffic in the souls of men for gain. They have learned Cain's "way" well.

Cain's system of worship had no room for the true God. Cain's "way" exchanged the knowledge of God with a lie. With the knowledge of God removed, man was free to serve himself, to make himself god. Paul clearly states the mind of unregenerate men.

Rom. 1:25 Who changed the truth of God into a lie, and worshipped and served the creature more than the Creator, who is blessed for ever. Amen

CHAPTER 33

THE END OF CAIN'S CIVILIZATION

Cain's society reached great levels of advancement. Men of renown built marvelous wonders. A magnificent civilization soon overspread the earth as men began to travel across the face of the world. Yes indeed, man did reach a zenith of innovation and expansion, unparalleled even by today's standard.

In spite of their great intellect and ability, they still rejected God. They continued to rebel and refused the knowledge of God. They set up their own gods after their own lusts. Their godless "way" soon led to violence, just as did Cain's. Violence gripped mankind; it ran rampant throughout all the earth. Wherever the "way of Cain" went, brutality and cruelty grew. Just as Cain's "way" led him to murder, so this society began to murder and shed blood. The earth was turned into a field of carnage as men devoured each other in their wickedness. The same result that Cain experienced is experienced by all of mankind: hatred, violence, and death. Cain's "way" led to destruction and ruin. It led to acts of violence and murder, even against one's own brother. All those who follow in its path will be led to the very same end, death.

Gen. 6:5 And GOD saw that the wickedness of man was great in the earth, and that every imagination of the thoughts of his heart was only evil continually.

God sends a man named Enoch to this society. This Enoch was different than the Enoch of Cain's lineage. This Enoch trusted in God, walked with Him, and served Him. He is given a word from God to preach against the men of Cain's civilization.

**Jude 1:14-15 And Enoch also, the seventh from Adam, prophesied of these, saying, Behold, the Lord cometh with ten thousands of his saints,
To execute judgment upon all, and to convince all that are ungodly among them of all their ungodly deeds which they have ungodly committed, and of all their hard speeches which ungodly sinners have spoken against him.**

Enoch warned of God's judgment. Enoch is very clear as to how God views these men; they are ungodly. From their deeds to their speech, nothing good is to be found, nothing to be praised, nothing to be admired. No matter how technologically advanced they became, they were still sinners, being driven by the fruit of the knowledge of good and evil. There was no justice, no righteousness, no value in any of their "way".

As God looked upon this civilization, He saw rebellion, hatred, and violence. Cain's "way" had enveloped the entire world. There is a form of godliness in the "way of Cain" but this "way" was powerless. Paul tells us this.

2 Tim. 3:5 Having a form of godliness, but denying the power thereof: from such turn away.

The tree of the knowledge of good and evil bares fruit. This fruit was seen in the society that Cain built. Violence, rebellion, theft, fornication, murder are just some of the manifestations of this fruit. We see this fruit everyday on the news and in the newspaper. The end result of man's attempt to be god is death; death to the land, death to culture, death to man himself. **Cain's "way" does not lead to paradise, it does not create a utopian society of peace and joy. The end of Cain's "way" is violence and death.**

When God looked upon the earth He saw that it was filled with violence. The reason that God gives for this violence is that man had corrupted His "way".

Gen. 6: 12 And God looked upon the earth, and, behold, it was corrupt; for all flesh had corrupted his way upon the earth.

God's "way" was there for men to follow but they did not, they followed another "way", a "way" that replaced God with man. This was the result of the tree of knowledge of good and evil, it corrupted God's "way", and it changed the truth of God into a lie. The verse states that all flesh followed after another "way".

This society, built upon the "way of Cain", became so violent and evil, that God judged it with Noah's flood. This was the end of the great society that Cain built, that was established upon his "way".

Gen. 6:13 And God said unto Noah, The end of all flesh is come before me; for the earth is filled with violence through them; and, behold, I will destroy them with the earth.

Only Noah and his family are saved. Noah is a man of faith. Noah is spared the judgment of God, because he had faith in God. It was only Noah who found grace in the eyes of the Lord, and that was because he alone followed after God's "way".

A society dedicated to the worshipping of the creature resulted in the destruction of all living creatures save one family. Death did come from that tree in the garden; a watery grave caused that world to perish. All their advancements and achievements were drowned. Their industries, markets, and arts all succumbed to the thunderous rain from heaven. Their wicked ways buried in the muck and mire that swallowed them all.

The seeds of Cain's "way" survived the flood and were planted in the new world. Noah's sons and daughters in-law were all eyewitnesses to the grandeur that once was. As they stepped into the new world their hearts desired the old world, the one that God judged. They are the bridge that crossed the flood waters, the link to the past. Through them, man again was indoctrinated into the "way of Cain". His "way" was planted and took root in the flourishing new society. Ever since, Cain's influence has again reigned in all of man's societies and cultures. Cain's "way" has reached into every civilization as man eats of Cain's fruit, tastes his doctrines, and follows his "way".

2 Pet. 3:7 But the heavens and the earth, which are now, by the same word are kept in store, reserved unto fire against the day of judgment and perdition of ungodly men.

Our world today is condemned and awaiting the wrath of God. Just as Cain's world was judged by water in Noah's flood, so its offspring is waiting to be judged by fire. We are living in a world waiting to be judged and punished for its wickedness. Our world is just as ungodly as Cain's was, and it's just as violent. This is the result of his "way".

CHAPTER 34

CONCLUSION

Cain was not an innocent victim of a whimsical God. He was not simply a man that lost his temper and murdered his brother. He was not unjustly condemned.

The light of scripture has revealed Cain's true character and his "way". Cain has been exposed and revealed as the scriptures portray him. **Cain was a Pharisee, a religious zealot, who perfectly embodied all that unbelief could produce.**

Cain's real evil is not only found in the murder of his brother, but in the "way" he established. It was this "way" that brought him to kill his brother. The "way of Cain" is satanic. It worships at the tree of the knowledge of good and evil, eating of its fruit. Cain's "way" usurps God's "way" and makes man his own god. It is a "way" that views man as "good", that worships the creature more than the Creator. Cain's "way" continues to guide billions of people to their eternal death and destruction.

The "way of Cain" does not produce the life and peace that it promises. Nor does it bring joy and tranquility to the world. No! The fruit of Cain corrupts everything it touches; it destroys terribly. It brings ruin, violence, and carnage everywhere it goes. The "way of Cain" is a murderous "way" that is led by murderous men.

Matt. 23:35 That upon you may come all the righteous blood shed upon the earth, from the blood of righteous Abel unto the blood of Zacharias son of Barachias, whom ye slew between the temple and the altar.

Christ told the Pharisees that it was they, and men of their "generation", whom He holds responsible for Abel's murder and the murders all the righteous since the beginning of time. This includes the blood of Stephen as well as those he mentions in Acts 7:51-52. This also includes the blood of those that we find in Hebrews.

Heb. 11:36-37 And others had trial of cruel mockings and scourgings, yea, moreover of bonds and imprisonment:
They were stoned, they were sawn asunder, were tempted, were slain with the sword: they wandered about in sheepskins and goatskins; being destitute, afflicted, tormented;

What a fearful and awful indictment by God the Son against the "way of Cain". God will accuse, judge, and condemn all who are religious, self-righteous, prideful, seekers of good works, "good" men, to the Lake of Fire.

In spite of God's judgment, men continue in their unbelief and rebellion against God, just as Cain did. Men have not heeded, listened to, or learned from God's destruction of those that first followed Cain's "way".

Cain's spirit is alive and well and exists everywhere. Every tribe, village, city, and culture is shaped and molded by Cain's "way". It reaches into every jungle, mountain, desert, island, and plain. It is found in places of worship, schools, colleges, libraries, museums, and seminaries; for these all teach and proclaim the "way of Cain". These all proclaim a gospel of self-righteousness.

The "way of Cain" flourishes today in man's/Cain's religious system. Cain's "religious industry" is powerful, influential, and holds men in darkness. Billions are in its grip. It has priesthoods, clergy, clerics, doctorates, professors, talk show personalities, gurus, Popes, Ayatollahs, Mullahs, Imams, Shamans, etc., as its leaders. Cain's "way" has wealth untold, buildings, steeples, candles, tapestries, sanctuaries, robes, altars, communion cups, the Eucharist, masses, ceremonies, confessions, beads, altars, baptisms, books, statues, signs, trinkets, holy water, palms, symbols, initiations, and the list goes on and on, limited only by man's evil imagination. Cain's "way" comes under many different names such as Hinduism, Buddhism, Islam, Orthodox, Jehovah's Witness, Mormonism, Druidism, Catholicism, Taoism, education, intellectualism, positive thinking, eastern mysticism, communism, socialism, spiritualism, there is no end. They all appear to be different but they all originate from the same root, the "way of Cain", and are all built upon the tree of the knowledge of good and evil. They all deny the blood of Christ as sufficient payment for sin.

Cain's "way" is determined to reign supreme. To this end it has initiated a war against all those who stand opposed to this "way". Beginning with the murder of Abel, the church of Cain seeks to silence, obliterate, and destroy the true church of God. Cain will use any and all means possible to be the victor. The "way of Cain" is a brutal dictator that is seditious, arrogant, and vehemently attempts to force all men to bow before it. There is no tolerance of God's faithful, no space for God's Word, no place for God, even though a key word in this "way" is tolerance. Their tolerance is inclusive of everything but God.

Prov. 14:12 There is a way which seemeth right unto a man, but the end thereof are the ways of death.

Jude 11a Woe unto them! For they have gone in the way of Cain

Appendix A

The Mark of Cain

Gen. 4:15   And the LORD said unto him, Therefore whosoever slayeth Cain, vengeance shall be taken on him sevenfold. And the LORD set a mark upon Cain, lest any finding him should kill him.

The Lord set a mark upon Cain so that Cain could be easily identified, and not killed. This mark was to cause men to stay away from him, as he was to be a wanderer; he was to live in isolation.

In disobedience to God, men embraced Cain along with his knowledge, wisdom, mark, and "way". They made Cain their leader and high priest. Cain avoided the isolation that the mark was intended to bring.

With Cain's acceptance, he was now free to use the mark to his advantage, something that God never intended for him to do. Cain perverted God's purpose of the mark. Cain used it for his good by causing men to believe that he had God's blessing and protection. They couldn't touch him.

If any man approached Cain, He could say, "You cannot kill me for I have the protection of God". Cain could show his mark as a witness to the fact that he indeed did have God's protection. **Cain perverted God's purpose of the mark by changing it to mean that it was a blessing from God.** Through Cain's corruption, the mark now represents something good that brings protection from harm and evil.

An example of this is seen with Lamech. Lamech claimed this protection based on Cain's mark when he too kills.

Gen. 4:23-24 And Lamech said unto his wives, Adah and Zillah, Hear my voice; ye wives of Lamech, hearken unto my speech: for I have slain a man to my wounding, and a young man to my hurt.
If Cain shall be avenged sevenfold, truly Lamech seventy and sevenfold.

Lamech kills, he claimed the same protection that Cain's mark brought to Cain. Lamech claimed this protection for himself. It was never God's intention for men to take this mark and use it as Lamech did. This example shows that the protection provided by Cain's mark has now been expanded to include others.

Those in Cain's society used the mark that was intended for Cain alone. It was used to provide blessing and protection as seen with Lamech.

Many have questioned as to just what this mark is. It is not my purpose to speculate as to what it is, but this one thing can be sure, Cain perverted God's purpose for it and incorporated it into his "way". This mark has continued throughout all of time and has been accepted by mankind as an important component of religion, the "way of Cain".

Appendix B

A defense for Adam?

Some have attempted to make excuses for Adam's eating of the fruit. Seeking to remove some of the blame from man and thereby transferring it to God.

Some claim, in defense of Adam and Eve, that they were deceived and that they did not totally understand what death really was. By implication, this would make God unjust in condemning Adam and Eve because He was not clear enough or did not provide enough information.

God answers those who seek to defend Adam and Eve; He shuts the mouths of all who want to find an excuse for man's rebellion. The scriptures shed more light and give further insight into the thoughts and actions of that event. It is Paul who provides the needed information.

I Tim. 2:14 And Adam was not deceived, but the woman being deceived was in the transgression.

According to this verse Adam could not claim that he was deceived. Eve could claim she was deceived but Adam could not. The implications of this statement remove all defenses for Adam. He stands without excuse, completely guilty.

Before they ate of the fruit, Adam and Eve did not consider themselves as naked. God had provided a covering for them. Some have speculated that perhaps they were clothed in light, but whatever it was, they had a covering provided by God.

Adam was with Eve when she ate the fruit, but she bit first. It is important to note that Eve ate first and then she gave to Adam. The reason that God says that Adam was not deceived is because Adam saw something happen to Eve after she bit. Adam saw Eve become naked. He saw the covering that God had provided removed from Eve as she spiritually died before his eyes. And in spite of what he saw, he bit anyway. He could not claim that he was deceived for he saw the result that that fruit had on Eve.

Adam made up his mind that he was going to be ruler, judge, and god no matter what the cost. Eve was tricked, but Adam was fully aware, he saw the consequences before he ate.

Some have also claimed that Adam bit because he loved Eve and therefore he ate in order to be with her, but this is not true. If Adam truly loved Eve he would have sought her best interest, for that is what love does. First, he would have attempted to prevent her from biting the fruit; and second, after she bit it, he should have thrown the fruit to the ground not eating of it himself and taken Eve by the hand and led her back to God. There Adam could have asked God what to do, maybe to undue or fix what she had done.

This is what Adam should have done; he should have taken her to the Lord and disavowed her actions. Trusting in the Lord to provide a remedy. Under the law, God made a provision for a husband to help his wife. If a wife made a vow that the husband knew was wrong he could have it disavowed.

Num. 30:6-8 And if she had at all an husband, when she vowed, or uttered ought out of her lips, wherewith she bound her soul;
And her husband heard it, and held his peace at her in the day that he heard it: then her vows shall stand, and

her bonds wherewith she bound her soul shall stand.
But if her husband disallowed her on the day that he
heard it; then he shall make her vow which she vowed,
and that which she uttered with her lips, wherewith she
bound her soul, of none effect: and the LORD shall
forgive her.

Num. 30:12-13 But if her husband hath utterly made
them void on the day he heard them; then whatsoever
proceeded out of her lips concerning her vows, or
concerning the bond of her soul, shall not stand: her
husband hath made them void; and the LORD shall
forgive her.
Every vow, and every binding oath to afflict the soul, her
husband may establish it, or her husband may make it
void.

Adam did not protest Eve's actions; he did not seek to undo
what she had done, he did not bring her to the Lord. He
instead concurred and confirmed what she had done.

Num. 30:14 But if her husband altogether hold his peace
at her from day to day; then he establisheth all her vows,
or all her bonds, which are upon her: he confirmeth
them, because he held his peace at her in the day that he
heard them.

Therefore Adam is responsible for the fall of mankind, he
had no excuse; he saw the outcome and still rebelled. Thus
Adam brought sin into the world and he is the one
responsible. God holds Adam responsible and not Eve for sin
and death.

Rom. 5:18 Therefore as by the offence of one judgment
came upon all men to condemnation; even so by the
righteousness of one the free gift came upon all men unto

justification of life.

Appendix C

Believers Who Go Back to the "Way of Cain"

The "way of Cain" is a "way" opposed to God. It is a "way" walked by all those who refuse to believe God's word. But unfortunately there are many saved men who having once left Cain's "way", becoming believers, return to follow it again.

When a believer ignores God's word he will fall victim to endless errors and be led back to the "way of Cain". Eternal salvation will not be lost to those believers who return to Cain's "way", for once a man receives God's righteousness as a gift, it is his forever, he can never lose it. But this believer will no longer stand for the truth, but will oppose it.

Saints that Paul had taught and cared for forsook him. Saints that worked side by side with him now stood contrary to him.

Phil. 3:18 For many walk, of whom I have told you often, and now tell you even weeping, that they are the enemies of the cross of Christ:

It grieved Paul's heart to see many of his brothers and sisters in the Lord return to a "way" opposed to God. He sheds tears of sorrow as once beloved saints, who stood for the grace of God, now became his enemy.

Paul also warned the elders at Ephesus of this.

Acts 20:29-30 For I know this, that after my departing shall grievous wolves enter in among you, not sparing the flock.

162

Also of your own selves shall men arise, speaking perverse things, to draw away disciples after them.

Paul states that believers, it will be some of them, who will bring harm and division to the church. They will leave the gospel of Christ and seek to establish themselves as the authority. They will seek to draw men away from the truth and turn them to their own doctrines and teachings. They will leave the faith and follow after their own lusts and desires; they go back to Cain.

This happens under the cloak of godliness. They claim they are doing the Lord's work but they are not. They are instead filling themselves with themselves. They have elevated their pride and listen to their foolish hearts. This is truly a blight on the Body of Christ, when those who once had faith now become carnal in their thinking and follow after their own hearts desires.

Paul again comments that some believers will depart from it.

1 Tim. 4:1- Now the Spirit speaketh expressly, that in the latter times some shall depart from the faith, giving heed to seducing spirits, and doctrines of devils;

When one leaves the scriptures he has nowhere to go but to himself and the Devil. They become his emissaries caring about his will seeking to further the darkness of Satan. For when the light is rejected there only remains darkness.

2 Tim. 2:25-26 In meekness instructing those that oppose themselves; if God peradventure will give them repentance to the acknowledging of the truth;
And that they may recover themselves out of the snare of the devil, who are taken captive by him at his will.

Believers who return to following Cain oppose themselves.

Believers who have returned to their flesh, who fulfill their own desires, who follow after Cain become despisers of God. They resist correction and rebuking. They instead will attack and defame the righteous, just as Cain did. It is very sad to see a saint behave in a way that is not consistent with who God has made him to be.

Suffering at the hands of the lost is bad enough, but it is all the more sorrowful when one suffers at the hands of a saint that has returned to following Cain, returned to follow his own pride and thoughts. They too when rebuked will lash out and seek to harm you. There is no end to what they will destroy: reputation, family, job, home, ministry etc... They must destroy you to save their pride, just like Cain.

Grace, forgiveness, and peace are all forgotten but hatred, unforgiveness, a hardened heart are the attitudes of these men. They will hold grudges, they will seek to have dominion over others declaring that their word should reign, laying aside the word of God. They will not be moved by the verses but will instead move to silence those who stand against them.

The scriptures tell us how to deal with this. If they will not accept correction they are to be avoided.

Rom. 16:17 Now I beseech you, brethren, mark them which cause divisions and offences contrary to the doctrine which ye have learned; and avoid them.

Just as the men in Cain's time should have avoided Cain, saints are to avoid believers who have been thus marked as God ordains.

To contact the author please visit the web site:

http://www.grace-harbor-church.org

There you will also find material for both children and adults including free Bible studies and downloadable messages from the author.